Traces

▼

Early Peoples of North Dakota

Barbara Handy-Marchello

and

Fern E. Swenson

TRACES

Early Peoples of North Dakota

Barbara Handy-Marchello

and

Fern E. Swenson

State Historical Society of North Dakota

Bismarck

2018

Cover ▶ Beacon Island painting by Greg Harlin

Book design and layout ▶ Lucy Annis Ganje

Map and timeline design ▶ Amy C. Bleier

Artifact photo editing ▶ Meagan Schoenfelder and Lorna Meidinger

Printer ▶ United Printing, Bismarck

Copyright © 2018 by the State Historical Society of North Dakota, 612 East Boulevard Avenue, Bismarck

All right reserved. No part of this publication may be reproduced, stored in a retrieval system, or transmitted, in any form or by any means, electronic, mechanical, photocopying, recording, or otherwise, without written permission of the copyright owner.

ISBN 978-1-891419-22-5

Library of Congress

Cataloging-in-Publication Data

Traces: Early Peoples of North Dakota. Bismarck, ND: State Historical Society of North Dakota, 2018.

128 p,: col ill., col. Maps; 28 cm.

Traces: Early Peoples of North Dakota publication was made possible with the generous contributions of:

PaleoCultural Research Group

U.S. Forest Service, Department of Agriculture

Dr. Fred Schneider

Table of Contents

Page	
5	List of Maps
6	Foreword
8	Introduction
Chapter 1 — 12	Artists in Stone: Paleoindians in North Dakota
Chapter 2 — 28	Great Innovations: The Plains Archaic Era
Chapter 3 — 44	Influences from the East: Plains Woodland Cultures
Chapter 4 — 68	People of the Earthlodges: Plains Village Cultures
Chapter 5 — 94	Bison, Horses, and International Trade: The Equestrian Tradition and Fur Trade Era
118	Conclusion
120	Illustration Credits
126	Acknowledgements
127	Further Reading

List of Maps

Page	
12	1.1 North Dakota glaciation, 11,500 BC
14	1.2 Migration route, 11,500 BC
17	1.3 Paleoindian sites
28	2.1 Archaic era sites
44	3.1 Plains Woodland era sites
50	3.2 Transcontinental trade routes
51	3.3 Besant and Sonota cultural areas
52	3.4 Hopewell cultural influence
67	3.5 Inundated communities, 1950s
68	4.1 Plains Village sites and lithic resource areas
70	4.2 Mandan, Hidatsa, and Arikara territories
70	4.3 Transcontinental trade routes
85	4.4 Location of Tribes, late 1700s
94	5.1 Fur Trade and Equestrian Era sites
97	5.2 Location of Tribes, early 1800s
108	5.3 Location of Tribes, 1850s and 1860s

Foreword

Traces
Early Peoples of North Dakota

Calvin Grinnell, Historian
Tribal Historic Preservation Office,
Mandan, Hidatsa and Arikara Nation

As an enrolled member of the Mandan, Hidatsa and Arikara Nation as well as a member of the State Historical Board of North Dakota, it is with immense pleasure that I introduce this comprehensive study of the native people on these Great Plains entitled Traces: Early Peoples of North Dakota. The staff and management of the State Historical Society of North Dakota compiled a noteworthy examination of lifeways developed over millennia across a vast ocean of prairie grassland etched by river valleys.

In these pages you will find myriad examples of human ingenuity adapting to an often-unforgiving environment. Long winters with below zero temperatures and record snowfalls several feet in depth coupled with summers of devastating droughts lasting several years are apparent even today. Unpredictable climate changes influenced the wanderings of the primary food source, huge bison herds rumbling across the Northern Plains searching for fresh pastures.

My Mandan, Hidatsa and Arikara ancestors used everything at their disposal to provide sustenance for their family and tribe, fashioning tools and weapons of stone, bone and wood. Every part of a bison carcass was used in some way. Knife River flint that was easily fashioned into razor-sharp arrow and spear points became a valuable commodity to many tribes. Our access to the flint quarries gave us a distinct advantage in trade with the nomadic peoples who visited our earthlodge villages near the mouth of the Knife River.

Native people understood the need to supplement their diet with the nutrients found in plant matter. Consequently, my people of the earthlodges found our niche in cultivating corn, beans, squash, and sunflowers on the fruitful bottomlands of the Missouri River trench. The excess harvest we used to establish a trade network that brought prosperity and access to trade goods from both coasts. Innovative practices like the atlatl and other technologies from far flung locales we incorporated into our culture.

Please take some time to reflect on this comprehensive archaeological treatise about my ancestors who populated these vast northern grasslands. You may be surprised by the resourceful strategies my people employed to successfully live in harmony with Grandmother Who Never Dies, the Hidatsas' name for Mother Earth. We believed she was married to Grandfather Snake who lived in the Missouri River. Together they provided nourishment and water, a necessity for all living creatures in our world.

We were grateful for the environment created for us by these beings and a whole host of other entities of the earth and sky. Complex ceremonies lasting several days were developed to show our respect for their generosity. We nurtured personal relationships with them, addressing them as elder relatives. We gave back by feasting them and offering personal sacrifices in return for their blessings: good harvests and weather, abundant medicines, and fortunate circumstances in defense of the villages.

It was a considerate understanding; as they took care of us, we acknowledged their help as a sign of respect. I believe native people are still here today because we still remember to be thankful for the greatest gift we were given: a beautiful land full of resources we can share.

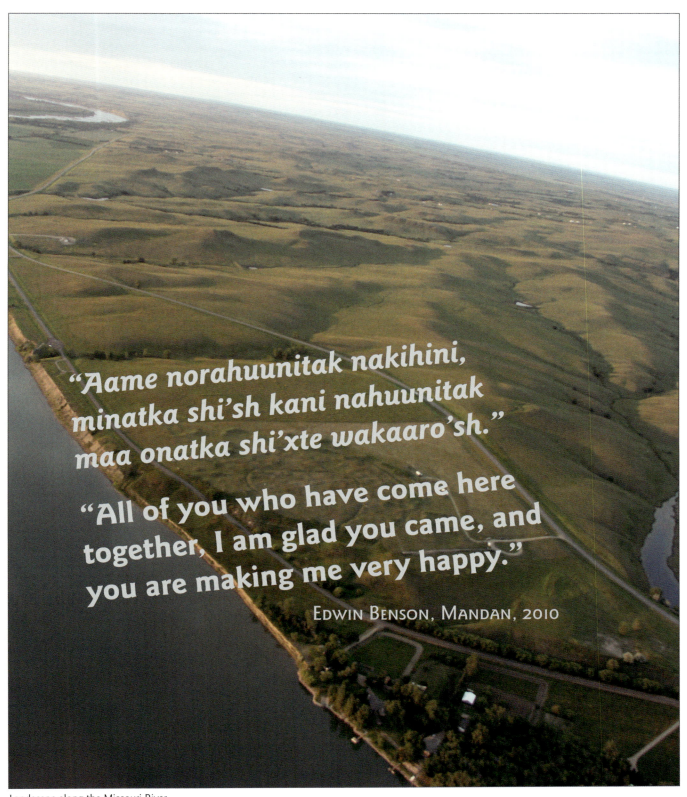

"*Aame norahuunitak nakihini, minatka shi'sh kani nahuunitak maa onatka shi'xte wakaaro'sh.*"

"All of you who have come here together, I am glad you came, and you are making me very happy."

EDWIN BENSON, MANDAN, 2010

Landscape along the Missouri River.

INTRODUCTION

Traces
Early Peoples of North Dakota

More than 13,000 years ago, some people traveling on foot from hilly country to the south and west came into North Dakota and prepared to hunt on the grass-covered plains west of the Little Missouri River. Since that long-past day, peoples of many different cultures have continued to come to North Dakota to find exactly what they wanted or needed. They stayed for a season or a lifetime. They lived comfortably by making whatever they needed from local resources. They found game and wild plants in abundance. They taught their children necessary skills and raised them to practice the traditions of their parents and grandparents while adapting new ideas from people of other cultures and developing innovative solutions to the problems they encountered. It is our good fortune that many of the people who lived here in the distant past left sufficient traces of their lives that we are able to understand how they lived and how this place both shaped and supported their lifeways.

Archaeologists have led the process of discovery and interpretation of cultures of the ancient past. While the story of ancient cultures in North Dakota is part of our state's history, the work of archaeologists is different from the work of historians. Each has a method of inquiry suitable to their disciplines. Historians examine the past through documents mostly written on paper. Their resources are recorded words, sometimes supplemented by pictures or objects. Archaeologists, however, work primarily with objects (artifacts) found on or in the ground. When archaeologists examine cultures that existed within an historic era, such as the nineteenth century Mandans, they use both archaeological materials and historic documents including artwork to conduct their studies. Both historians and archaeologists rely on oral histories to support their research.

Archaeologists draw on many disciplines. Their education begins with anthropology, the scientific study of human beings, but they specialize in the subfield of archaeology. In addition, archaeologists work with soil scientists, geologists, climatologists, chemists, zoologists, artists, and other specialists, and often develop their own expertise in one area including digital technology. This broad approach to archaeological study maximizes the information gained from each project.

Archaeologists, then, are scientists who apply methods honed by professional experience and practiced with care to locate and investigate the sites of camps and villages, bison kills, and stone quarries. In recent years, archaeologists have become skilled in the use of modern technological instrumentation and methods in order to "read" sub-surface evidence of human occupation. New technology has changed the nature of archaeological research just as new technology changed the way people worked thousands of years ago.

Through years of discovery, collection, and analysis of material evidence, archaeologists have developed ideas about past cultures and debated those ideas until they are either discarded or accepted. In this way, archaeologists piece together a fairly complete picture of life in different eras of the past. Though the evidence available at one site may not be complete, it is a piece of a puzzle that fits with other parts to reveal the larger picture of that time period or culture. In the same way, North Dakota's ancient cultures fit into the larger story of North American archaeology. Archaeologists track the exchange of tools and technologies to understand how people or cultural characteristics migrated across the continent.

Even though the state of North Dakota did not exist during any time period of the ancient past, this book uses modern state and county boundaries to define the particular area of interest that is part of a larger region now called the Northern Great Plains. The region, however, looked very different when people first arrived. Ice sheets (glaciers) still covered much of the eastern portion of North Dakota. Glacial Lake Agassiz, more than sixty miles wide at its highest level, receded for the last time around nine thousand years ago, leaving only the shallow Red River flowing through a flat plain. The Souris (Mouse) River looped down along a path cut by glaciers from Canada into North Dakota. These waterways developed as meltwater channels along the front edge of the receding glaciers. The James and Sheyenne rivers, rising in east-central North Dakota provided shelter, wood, water, and game for the groups of people who camped and hunted along the banks. The Missouri River which still flows between deep-cut banks from the western border through the center of the state, connected the Rocky Mountains with the Gulf of Mexico. In the thirteenth century, North Dakota's earliest villages were built along the banks of the river; by the nineteenth century, it was a thoroughfare for travelers of many native and immigrant cultures. The Little Missouri River cuts through the rough and rocky badlands on the western edge of the state creating habitat for game animals and edible plants in its deep canyons and grassy meadows.

In west-central North Dakota, in the valley of the Knife River and its major tributary, Spring Creek, a large deposit of high-quality flint lies just below the soil surface. This fine-grained stone, now called Knife River flint, was quarried here for thousands of years. It is likely that this and other quarries drew groups of people to the region because the stone had excellent qualities for knapping into dart points, knives, and other tools. Knife River flint was not the only stone available in North Dakota, but over thousands of years, different cultural groups preferred it to other types of stone because it is relatively easy to knap and because it holds a sharp edge.

Different types of stone and different ways of working it are important examples of archaeological evidence. One might say the worked stones that were once part of a Clovis-era toolkit are also an important part of an archaeologist's toolkit, but for very different reasons. A flintknapper's method of knapping, or chipping, stone and the final shape of a dart or arrow point when found hundreds or thousands of years later, provide clues to determine who knapped the tool and approximately when that person lived. However, one point does not tell a complete story. To learn the whole story, or as much as can possibly be gained from a site, the archaeologist has to consider the stone point in the context of the entire site.

Context consists of the arrangements of all the artifacts in a site. Archaeologists carefully examine a site, record observations, and make notes about all the details. They measure the depth of the soil at which most of the artifacts are found and the spacing of artifacts around the site. The characteristics of all bone, stone, shell, or metal objects—even the tiniest pieces—yield important information. Archaeologists look for depressions in the earth where it appears that someone once dug a hole or pit. Was the hole big enough for a house, deep enough for a cache, or long enough for a fortification ditch? Was there any charred wood or ash marking a hearth? Had the bones been cracked to remove marrow, or had they been gnawed by dogs? These questions and dozens more must be addressed as the site is examined. The context must be carefully recorded so that accurate data is available for later laboratory analysis. An ancient tool taken from a site without attention to context has no archaeological value.

The people who knapped projectile (spear, dart, or arrow) points drew on a body of technical skills and cultural traditions to manufacture a point that suited their needs. Knappers tended to choose a point style that was common among their peers. These point styles might have prevailed for hundreds of years and become associated with a particular culture. Years ago, archaeologists began the practice of naming points for the location where they were first found. Clovis points are, so far, the earliest named point in North America. They were first discovered near Clovis, New Mexico, but have since been found all over the continent. Archaeologists have also given the name Clovis to the culture of people who made these points, assuming that they shared many cultural characteristics in addition to the skills required to manufacture the Clovis-style point. As time passed, people of the Clovis culture chose to make points of a different style. This major cultural change is identified by a new name designating the new culture(s) and the time period of their existence.

Archaeologists use these two major organizing principles—chronology and technology—to analyze artifacts found in an archaeological site. Evidence such as projectile points or pieces of broken pottery can be classified according to manufacturing techniques, shape, decorative designs, location in soil layers, or association with organic material that can be dated or identified according to chemical or physical properties. However, chronology and technology assessments occasionally fail to answer all the questions raised by an archaeological site. That may be because the site was used over a long period of time by peoples of different cultures; or erosion, prairie fire, digging, or other disturbance damaged or displaced the evidence; or a particular group of people did not adopt the technology commonly used by others at that time. For the reader who is not a specialist, the fluid nature of archaeological classification can be confusing. If it seems complicated, and it is, just imagine how future archaeologists will struggle to understand human cultures in the twenty-first century based on the evidence we leave behind.

In this book, the chapters are organized chronologically according to the major archaeological time periods of North Dakota. Within the chapters cultures are identified by their technologies, traditions, and artifacts. However, you will often find the words "probably," "perhaps," and "possibly" describing ancient sites and the events that took place there. While archaeologists have made discoveries in recent years that have advanced our knowledge of the ancient past, there remain great opportunities for further research.

The dates associated with the five cultural traditions discussed in this book have been assigned in accordance with major events that affected the way people lived or with technologies or lifeways that mark a significant departure from previous cultural standards. For instance, the building of earthlodges in fortified villages where people cultivated corn and other crops marks the beginning of the Plains Village era when sedentary village life shaped the cultures the peoples of the Northern Great Plains, even those who did not settle in permanent villages. However, others in the region did not take up horticulture; they moved frequently and continued in the Woodland tradition. In the same way, the Plains Village tradition did not end with the era of the Equestrian tradition and fur trade, though it was significantly altered. The interactions of peoples coexisting with different lifeways allow us to think more holistically about the past.

Cultural periods are associated with date ranges that archaeologists generally agree on but, change from time to time when newly acquired evidence focuses new light on cultural change and causes a re-consideration of the time periods. Ancient peoples, however, complicated archaeologists' attempts at classification by maintaining old ways even when new technologies and lifeways were adopted by some of their neighbors. The timelines are an imperfect guide that help to organize information, but they are not rigid, and peoples of ancient times certainly never had any idea that their lives would be subject to some future concept of the passage of time.

It is important to note that dates of the cultural periods in North Dakota do not always coincide with the dates of a culture of the same name in other parts of North America. The period associated with peoples of the Woodland cultures began much earlier in the Ohio River valley than in the James River valley. The dates of Northern Great Plains cultures are associated with the time period when significant cultural characteristics appeared, not by arbitrary calendar dates.

Today, we consider ourselves forward-looking people whose technology changes rapidly. Why should we bother to examine the distant past when ancient technologies underwent very little change for hundreds of years? There are several answers to that question. Ancient peoples were like us in many ways. They devised technologies to solve their everyday problems of acquiring food and shelter, managing transportation, and securing the safety of their families. They cared for their children and taught them the skills they would need as adults. They were concerned about personal appearance and adorned themselves with beads and pendants of beautiful, hard-to-find materials. Their spiritual beliefs helped them understand their lives and the world in which they lived.

We can learn a lot from the ancients. They were highly skilled and hard-working people—they had to be in order to survive. Their curiosity led them to discover new foods and new ways to prepare food for their families. They were innovators who developed new skills and technologies that brought greater comfort and security to their families and communities. When the climate changed from cold to warm, or from wet to dry, affecting where they lived and what they hunted, they adapted. When travelers arrived, they often welcomed them and embraced the new ideas and materials the strangers brought with them. In other words, even thousands of years after the first humans arrived in North Dakota, we can see that there is much to admire in these ancient peoples and that we share many cultural values.

As ancient peoples moved about North Dakota's prairies, badlands, and waterways, they left behind traces of their presence. During the twentieth century, many of the sites where ancient peoples lived or hunted were identified and some have become state- or federally-administered historic sites. Double Ditch, Huff, and Menoken are among several state historic sites related to ancient cultures that have been investigated by archaeologists and are now protected from development. The Lynch Knife River Flint Quarry is now a National Historic Landmark. Knife River Indian Villages National Historic Site where Lewis and Clark met Mandan and Hidatsa Indians in 1804 is managed by the National Park Service and open to the public. The Biesterfeldt Site is administered by the Archaeological Conservancy. Visitors to public archaeological sites can see how people lived on the North Dakota prairies long ago.

This book is designed to complement the exhibits in the State Museum's Innovation Gallery: Early Peoples, in the North Dakota Heritage Center in Bismarck. These exhibits were developed in coordination with Native American expertise and advice from each of the tribal nations in North Dakota. Many of the objects pictured in these pages are on display in the exhibits. In the exhibit hall, you can listen to the spoken, native language version of the quotations that introduce each section of the exhibit and learn more about language revitalization efforts. This book provides more complete information on the lifeways of ancient peoples and explanation of archaeological methods used in locating and interpreting the archaeological sites of North Dakota.

The Innovation Gallery: Early Peoples at the North Dakota Heritage Center and State Museum in Bismarck.

CHAPTER 1

ARTISTS IN STONE

Paleoindians in North Dakota
11,500 to 5500 BC

Lone Man was walking along and
became aware of himself.
The land was new
where he was going.

Numak Maxana kasimira mako'sh.
Ishkaha waaiksaho mako'sh.
I'ima maake kitahini ro ores unta.

– Mandan Origin Story

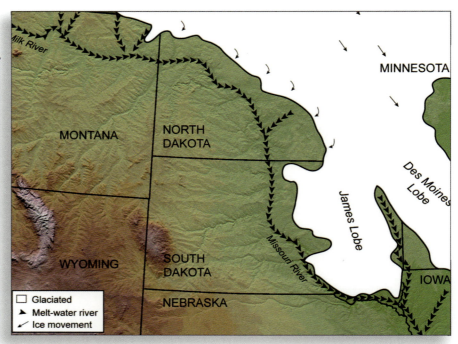

MAP 1.1. Glaciers pushed into North Dakota several times over thousands of years. They reshaped the surface of the land and left lakes and rivers as the great ice sheets retreated.

Illustration by *Greg Harlin—
Wood Ronsaville Harlin, Inc.*

Thirteen thousand, five hundred years ago or so, before the last of the Laurentide ice sheets (glaciers) departed North Dakota, and before Glacial Lake Agassiz was reduced to a shallow river now called the Red River of the North, a group of people left a large cache of stone bifaces near present-day Beach, North Dakota. Archaeologists have identified these people as part of the "Clovis" cultural tradition. Clovis is one of many cultures classified as Paleoindian. Distinctive Clovis artifacts have been found across North America. Other than evidence of their stone working technology, we don't know who they were or what they called themselves, what language they spoke, or how many were in their group. We don't know why they were here or what they planned to do. The "don't knows" loom large over this site, but even a small collection of bifaces (stones that have been partially shaped by removing flakes from both surfaces) can tell us quite a lot about the first humans known to have set foot in North Dakota.

These stones constitute a significant body of evidence to archaeologists. From these artifacts, we learn that people who used a technology that archaeologists have named Clovis to shape stones into useful weapons and tools spent some time in North Dakota. They might have lit a small fire, or perhaps a burning tree fell near their caches. Using the charcoal left by this fire, archaeologists have applied carbon dating techniques to determine that the cache was prepared 13,500 years ago. This date makes Beach one of the earliest known Clovis caches in North America.

Mastodons became extinct in North America a few hundred years after people cached their bifaces near Beach. It is possible that they hunted mastodons in this region.
Illustration by *Greg Harlin—Wood Ronsaville Harlin, Inc.*

The bifaces, found in several pits each about the size of a volleyball, are made of at least nine types of stone. Some quartzite and chert came from the Hartville Uplift, also known as Spanish Diggings, in present-day southeastern Wyoming about 330 miles from Beach. Some silicified wood came from West Rainy Butte, about fifty-two miles from Beach. Most of the bifaces, fifty-eight pieces, were made from stone found only ten miles away at Sentinel Butte. This White River Group Silicate (also known as WRGS or Chadron formation chert) can be found in a wide area on the Central and Northern Great Plains. However, further scientific testing demonstrated that the WRGS found on Sentinel Butte is distinct from other silicates of this type, so we know that the people who made the Beach caches gathered nodules for these preforms (bifaces) at nearby Sentinel Butte. The geographic origin of

THE TIME FACTOR

How do we know how much time people saved by preparing the bifaces for the Beach cache? Archaeologists who do stone knapping and are familiar with the land and terrain near Beach have estimated how much time was saved by bringing stone from Sentinel Butte to the Beach site, knapping it into 58 useful bifaces, and storing it in the caches.

It takes about 15 minutes to climb up Sentinel Butte and 15 minutes to climb down. Locating good-sized pieces of chert (including White River Group Silicate) might have taken 10 minutes per piece for a total of 9.7 hours. The time to walk from Sentinel Butte to the Beach cache site was about 5.4 hours. Assuming 15 to 30 minutes to knap each stone into a biface, if the stone did not break badly and the stone knapper made no mistakes, it took 9 to 14.5 hours to manufacture 58 bifaces.

The total time needed to locate, transport, and knap 58 bifaces was 30 to 45 man-hours. If four people worked at this process, it would take 6 to 9.5 hours. While the knappers were acquiring the stone, transporting it, and knapping the stone into bifaces, someone else was watching the children, preparing the meals, and doing any number of tasks to keep the group fed, healthy, and sheltered. It was a good day's work for a small group of people, but at the end of the day, they were prepared to hunt when the opportunity arose.

This biface, discovered in the Beach cache, was sharpened on both sides as shown by the small knicks in the edges.

MAP 1.2. The people who made the biface cache near Beach had traveled from eastern Wyoming through South Dakota bringing stones from those areas to Beach.

Archaeologists create a grid (white string) of a site before carefully digging. This archaeologist is brushing dirt away from a stone in the Beach cache. *Photo courtesy of Bruce B. Huckell, University of New Mexico*

the stones in the cache tells us that this group of people had traveled through the Central and Northern Great Plains, moving steadily from south to north. Studies at other Clovis sites around the continent suggest this migration pattern from south toward the northeast was common, perhaps to take advantage of springtime warming trends.

As archaeologists try to understand why this cache was created in this particular place, they have made several assumptions based on logic, their knowledge of Clovis culture, and the environment in which these people lived. It is important to understand first that the people were hunters. They hunted a variety of large mammals, especially mastodons and bison, and perhaps ancient horses and camels. Late in the Pleistocene epoch, these animals (known as megafauna) were becoming somewhat scarce and would become extinct within a few hundred years. For hunters, pursuing prey was a full-time occupation. They had to know what to expect of their prey and be prepared at all times to take quick advantage of opportunities to hunt. Hunters and their families were on the move nearly all the time. As they traveled, they picked up useful pieces of stone and worked them into bifaces and finished tools. They carried finished or nearly finished stone tools so they did not have to carry the weight of unworked rocks. There are perhaps two dozen known Clovis biface caches around the country—almost all discovered in what are or were grassland environments—which suggest that caching the bifaces was a common strategy employed to economize on the manpower and travel time needed for successful hunting.

When the people needed food and game animals could be found nearby, there was an urgent need to move quickly. If they needed to resupply their toolkit, it was to their great advantage to retrieve bifaces from a nearby cache. Archaeologists have estimated that preparing the fifty-eight WRGS bifaces found at Beach took between thirty and forty-five man-hours. When the hunt was eminent, hunters could access the stored bifaces very quickly and finish preparing the points. The Beach cache suggests that the people planned carefully for all aspects of their hunt for food.

Adjacent to the Beach cache was a small work area, where archaeologists found several flakes that had been used for cutting or scraping tasks. Flakes, pieces of stone removed in the processing of stone into tools, were often used for cutting or scraping tools. Sometimes called "expedient tools," they were picked up and used as needed. These simple tools were of the same materials as those in the cache. In addition, hundreds of small pieces of hematite (red iron ore) were scattered in this area. Hematite, when ground to a powder and mixed with water, produces a vibrant red paint. The Hartville Uplift area contains not only sources of stone but also large hematite deposits (also called iron mines). Might the hematite have been transported from Hartville? As yet, archaeologists are not certain.

Two important facts conclusively link the Beach cache to the Clovis cultural tradition. One is the date. The confirmed radiocarbon date (also called carbon dating or carbon-14 dating) of 13,500 years ago places the Beach cache among the earliest known sites of the Clovis tradition in North America. So far, there is no firm evidence of a stone tool technology that pre-dates Clovis, even though recent archaeological finds suggest that human occupation of North America may go back more than twenty-thousand years.

This biface displays overshot flaking extending from the upper left to lower right.

The other important fact is the technique used in producing these preforms or bifaces. Clovis tool knappers were experts in shaping stone by overshot flaking, a method requiring great skill. The stone worker had to strike the stone with an antler or another stone in such a way as to remove a large flake (stone chip) across the biface, running from one side to the other. In further refinement, the edges were tapered and sharpened on both sides to create a sharp point. Even though the tools in the Beach cache are unfinished and do not feature fluting (a central groove or channel in the base of both faces of the projectile point) indicative of Clovis points, the overshot technique is known to be part of the process used to achieve the typical Clovis point. Overshot flaking is very difficult, and in the hands of someone who was less than expert, the stone might have broken into unusable fragments.

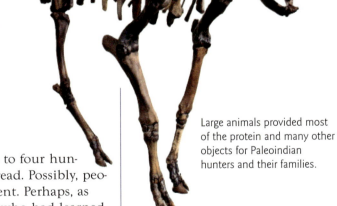

Large animals provided most of the protein and many other objects for Paleoindian hunters and their families.

Studies of Clovis sites all over North America, including the first one found near Clovis, New Mexico, tell us that Clovis weapons and tools were in use throughout the continent for about three to four hundred years. We can only guess how the technology spread. Possibly, people of the Clovis tradition migrated across the continent. Perhaps, as their communities grew in population, young people who had learned Clovis knapping (stone working) techniques moved to new locations. They might have engaged in extensive trading systems that spread the technology far and wide. Probably more than one of these possibilities helped distribute Clovis stone working techniques. Since the end of the Clovis cultural tradition, no other style of stone knapping has been as widely distributed. However, the usefulness of the Clovis technology eventually came to an end.

Naming the Lake Ilo Sites

When Lake Ilo was drained to repair the dam, exposing more than ten thousand years of human occupation, archaeologists had to organize the process of examination of the many sites and layers of occupation. The research on the Lake Ilo sites had to cover more than one-half mile east to west and just under a half mile north to south. When looking for tiny bits of broken bone and stone, this is a lot of territory to cover.

The area of Paleoindian occupation at Lake Ilo was divided into three main sites named Big Black, Young-Man-Chief, and Bobtail Wolf. These names were chosen to honor men of stature among the Hidatsas. Bobtail Wolf, who was present at the founding of Like-a-Fishhook Village in 1845, was descended from those who traditionally kept one of the Big Bird bundles. The rites performed by the holders of the Big Bird bundle were associated with flintknapping, and through these rituals a flintknapper received the authority to do this work. Holders of the Big Bird bundle were also empowered to perform rain rituals. Big Black and Young-Man-Chief were also holders of Big Bird bundles.

The archaeologists who began their work on these sites in 1993 found these names appropriate because they were working on very important sites where flintknapping took place. In addition, during the summer of that first year of work, frequent and heavy rain showers kept the research site muddy and nearly unworkable. Though the archaeologists chose Hidatsa names to identify the sites, they did not mean to imply that the people who camped at Bobtail Wolf were the ancestors of the Hidatsas who later settled along the Knife River. The name is simply to honor the Hidatsas, not to establish heritage.

Over time, Clovis points were replaced by new techniques for manufacturing stone projectile points and other tools; Goshen or Folsom points were next to appear. Archaeologists have debated why the change took place. Some believe an asteroid crashed into Earth resulting in the extinction of at least thirty-two species of Late Pleistocene (Ice Age) megafauna such as mammoths. Other scientists argue that humans hunted large mammals to extinction. Climate change also played a part in reducing the range and habitat of large Late Pleistocene animals. As the climate on the Northern Plains warmed, plant life adapted, resulting in extensive grasslands and causing a ripple of extinctions among the largest animals. Very likely, several events, as yet unknown, coincided to bring about a change in the plant and animal life of North America. As the climate warmed, bison (*Bison antiquus*), elk, deer, pronghorn, and smaller animals such as rabbits, beavers, and a great variety of birds, fish, and amphibians adapted and thrived. There is evidence that all of these animals, but especially bison, contributed to the diet of the Paleoindian cultures that came after the people of the Clovis tradition. Clovis-style projectile points became obsolete in a changed world.

Knife from Beach cache

The Goshen culture appeared after Clovis and may have coincided in time with Folsom culture. Some Goshen points have been found in North Dakota, but evidence of Folsom cultural groups in North Dakota present a far more complete picture of Paleoindian life.

Manufacturers of Folsom points made their way into North Dakota about 10,500 years ago. Some archaeologists claim that the Folsom style point was first developed on the Northern Great Plains. If true, then somewhere in a region several hundred miles across, people living in an environment requiring different weapons and tools than their ancestors had used, developed a new technique for knapping stone. Folsom, as the new technology is now called, required different, but no less demanding, skills in striking and shaping stone into a useful tool. Folsom points tend to be smaller than Clovis points, but they still have the distinctive flute or central channel through the center of the point. Fluted points are thinner in the middle which makes it easier to haft (attach) them to a spear or dart. Folsom points, however, are longer than the flutes on Clovis points, nearly reaching the tip on both faces of the point. The new point style must have met the needs of the people. Perhaps they found it easier to make and attach to a spear, or it made a more effective weapon on the animals they usually hunted.

Folsom point

While there is evidence of Folsom camps or quarries in several places around the state, it now appears that a place between the shores of Spring Creek and Murphy Creek in present-day Dunn County was a favorite place to gather. Today, this area is part of Lake Ilo National Wildlife Refuge in west-central North Dakota. But at least 12,500 years ago (10,500 BC), this was a lively spot that hosted camps of people who manufactured projectile points in the Folsom tradition.

Before the dam formed Lake Ilo in the 1930s, this was the location where Murphy Creek joined Spring Creek. The creeks flowed through sagebrush and grass-covered prairie. Nearby draws held junipers, birch and alder trees, hazelnut shrubs, and a variety of fruit-bearing bushes. Pines might have been found on the ridges. The grass was lush and attracted plenty of wildlife. Just below the ground surface, was a good supply of Knife River flint, perhaps the most important element drawing people to this location.

Buffalo berries *(Shepherdia argentea)* are native to North Dakota. They produce nutritious, tart berries in late summer. *Photo by Provincial Archives of Alberta*

In 1989, when the lake was drained in order to make repairs to the dam, several archaeological sites were found in the lakebed. Three of these sites, Bobtail Wolf, Young-Man-Chief, and Big Black, have revealed multiple occupations by people who used Folsom technology. Because occupation at these sites was intense and recurred over hundreds of years, archaeologists have extracted a great deal of information about the people who lived here.

Both Big Black and Bobtail Wolf camps were most likely established in the summer. We don't know how long the people stayed; the length of the encampment may have varied for each group. However, there is good evidence that they stayed long enough to prepare a substantial supply of tools and weapons for future hunts.

MAP 1.3. Paleoindian sites and location of lithic resources.

The people who came here probably traveled from areas to the south and west. They brought some stone with them from Rainy Butte (sixty-two miles southwest) and porcellanite from the badlands west of Spring Creek. The people picked up Knife River flint cobbles (pieces of stone) along Spring Creek to forge into tools to replenish their toolkit.

At Big Black and Bobtail Wolf, the people conducted all the activities of summer; they hunted, made tools, and probably socialized with other groups gathered at this perfect summer place. This was, however, not a place for a big hunt. Bones and teeth suggest that hunters took advantage of the occasional passing bison herd to kill and butcher only one or two animals, just enough for daily needs.

Knife River flint is found only in North Dakota. A large quarry is located a few miles north and east of Lake Ilo. This distinctive flint was highly valued for its knapping qualities.

TRACES ▶ EARLY PEOPLES OF NORTH DAKOTA | 17

Darts or spears were made from wood, bone, or antler that was straightened with a spokeshave. This stone tool was shaped to curve over the shaft of the dart.

We do not know the exact method of the hunt. Did they drive the animals into a surround or corral where they were trapped and then killed? Did they ambush bison at a waterhole? Or did they, as some have suggested, find weakened animals already near death, and finish them off with their weapons? The hunters brought the entire carcass back to camp, probably transporting it in pieces. They processed the meat using stone knives and used stone scrapers to clean the hides for different uses.

The most important activity at these camps was the gathering of Knife River flint and the manufacturing of as many as thirty different kinds of tools. The people picked up cobbles large enough to process into projectile points, knives, scrapers, gravers and burins (tools for engraving or marking stone or bone), hammerstones, and many other kinds of tools. Sources of Knife River flint were found not only at Bobtail Wolf and Big Black, but to the east along Spring Creek.

Foreshafts, spears and an atlatl

In order to make a functional weapon from a stone point, hunters hafted projectile points onto the foreshaft of a dart by wrapping a length of prepared wet sinew around the joint; as it dried, it created a secure bond. The sinew was made from a ligament or tendon of one of the animals that had been butchered for meat. The weapon-maker used a piece of bone, antler, or wood, straightened with a stone spokeshave, to make the foreshaft. The foreshaft was then attached to the longer main spear shaft, most likely made of wood. This arrangement allowed the foreshaft to break off if the point became lodged in a bone, or if the tip broke off the point. The hunter was able to retrieve a part of his weapon and repair it for further use.

Hunting involved efforts of an entire family group. Though archaeologists are not sure about the division of labor, it is likely that men killed the animals while women, using sharp-edged, stone knives cut the meat into strips for drying. *Pembina State Museum, SHSND*

Foreshaft materials such as bone and antler were hard and resisted the stone tools used to straighten them. The bone and antler wore out the stone tools rather quickly. However, the evidence for manufacture of foreshafts and spears gives us another view of the purpose of these campsites. Located near a good source of stone for making tools, people could make and replace worn tools as necessary while they replenished their toolkits. When they left this camp, they could carry biface preforms and other partially flaked pieces of stone with them for use in future tasks. Unlike the Clovis groups, however, people of the Folsom culture apparently did not cache stones or tools where they expected to return for them.

It appears to archaeologists that certain steps in the processing of tools were undertaken in specific places. Evidence suggests that, at least on some occasions, cobbles were shaped into preforms (also called blanks) at the Bobtail Wolf site, then transported to Big Black for finishing. It is not known whether this meant specialization in the different parts of the manufacturing process, or that manufacturing also involved spiritual rituals that had to be conducted in certain locations. Of course, it is also possible that the people took advantage of an opportunity to socialize while hammering on stone.

On the left is a cast of a Clovis projectile point. On the right is a Folsom projectile point. The Folsom point was manufactured with a flute, or channel, from the base to near the tip.

Some stone flakes found at Bobtail Wolf correspond to the manufacture of ultrathin bifaces. These tools required a sophisticated knapping technique that reduced a piece of Knife River flint to a wide, very thin, bi-concave tool. This knife was so thin that the depth or thickness of the point was equal to one-tenth or less of the width. It was very difficult to manufacture such a delicate tool, but people who were expert at Folsom technology seemed very capable of making them. Ultrathin bifaces had razor-sharp edges that could be resharpened several times. Some archaeologists suggest that women used ultrathin bifaces to cut bison meat into thin strips or to scrape flesh from raw hides; therefore, women may have manufactured these specialized tools. The ultrathin biface has been found only in Folsom sites so far, and may be a distinctive element of cultures that used Folsom technology.

Agate Basin technology produced a symmetrically tapered point without a flute. The light-colored edges on this point indicate patina, a process of aging on stone exposed to weather.

At the end of the summer stay at the Lake Ilo site, people had acquired enough Knife River flint, manufactured a sufficient supply of tools and weapons, and had, perhaps, replenished their supply of hides, dried meat, and plant foods. They then packed up their toolkits and set off on the next round in the annual cycle of seasonal activities. They headed out across the plains using and discarding tools along the Missouri River, the Souris (Mouse) River, and as far north as central Manitoba. Some people left Spring Creek and moved south or west with their new tools, leaving broken points and tools made of Knife River flint in eastern Wyoming and Montana. Nowhere else on their journeys would they find Knife River flint or any other stone with the fine qualities for knapping that characterized Knife River flint. And in

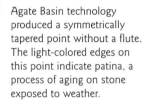

This ultra-thin tool was used as a cutting tool. Ultrathin bifaces had very sharp edges and were resharpened as needed. This may have been a tool used primarily by women.

How do we know?

What we know about the earliest Americans is based on archaeological evidence. First, the evidence must be discovered, and that often occurs by accident. Someone may stumble across a projectile point while on a hike, or a construction project may unearth evidence of human activity that took place hundreds or thousands of years ago.

The evidence, in the form of stone points, pieces of bone or stone tools, pottery, and sites of activity such as a bison kill or village, must, if possible, be carefully collected, studied, and preserved. Not only the artifacts, or material evidence, but the results of carbon dating, soil layer and type, as well as other physical and chemical tests must be considered.

Even with all the information that has accumulated since the early 20th century, we still have large gaps in our knowledge of the ancient past. Though archaeologists now think that humans were present on the North American continent more than 15,000 years ago, they do not know for certain when humans first arrived on the North American continent. While there is widespread agreement that people migrated to North America from Asia during the Ice Age over what was then a land bridge now called Beringia, there is some speculation that people might have used other pathways to occupy the American continents. As the human population became large enough to spread across the continent, the people left traces of their lives where they camped and hunted. Where climate and soil favored preservation, archaeologists have found enough evidence to draw some conclusions.

As new evidence appears, archaeologists add that to their knowledge. In the process, old ideas are discarded and new ideas are debated. The process will continue as new sites are located and scientific evaluation becomes more sophisticated.

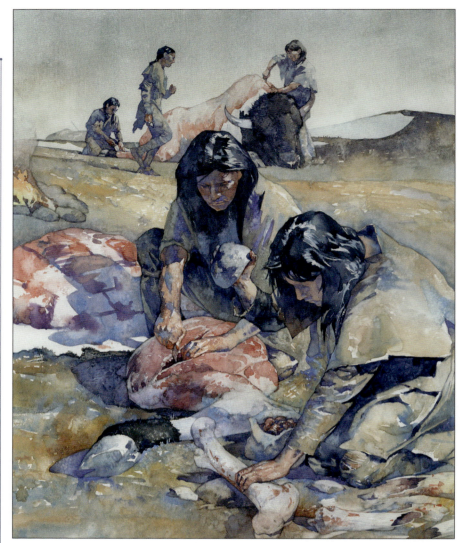

Bone marrow was an important source of calories and nutrition. Hunters broke the long bones of a bison carcass to remove the marrow. *Illustration by Greg Harlin—Wood Ronsaville Harlin, Inc.*

the centuries to come, no other people with a flintknapping tradition would manufacture stone tools of a quality equal to Folsom tools.

While we do not know much about seasonal activity, archaeologists have acquired enough information about the camps established by Paleoindians to make some broad statements. For instance, Paleoindians usually lived in small family-linked groups. From time to time, they formed larger multi-family social groups at places such as Bobtail Wolf. They moved often, and set up new camps where they could take advantage of needed resources. Winter camps might have been of longer duration, but not permanent. In winter camps, where almost every form of social, spiritual, and economic activity took place, the emphasis was on hunting.

A hunting site located in North Dakota gives us a good view of what winter might have been like for Paleoindians approximately 12,300 years ago (10,300 BC). This particular group found a nice hilltop on the north side of the Missouri River where they spotted a herd of bison. We don't know how they organized the hunt, but they might have driven the animals into an enclosure and killed them there. They killed at least twenty-nine animals and processed the carcasses just a few yards from the kill site. Today this site is within the boundaries of Lake Sakakawea and is known as Beacon Island.

It is important to note that this was not a camp. It was a place where hunters spent a day or two killing bison and processing meat for transport to their winter camp. How far that was, we don't know, but the hunters packed out the most valuable parts of the carcasses, leaving the heads and the lower part of the forelegs and hind legs as well as the backbones at the site. They probably took some organs as well; liver, heart, and other organ meats were rich sources of nutrition. They also used stone cobbles to break the long bones so they could remove the marrow. Bone marrow is high in fat and supplies important calories to support winter activity as well as other nutrients. The presence of predators, such as wolves, may have been the reason to hunt and butcher at a site some distance from the main camp. The hunters would have wanted to avoid predators that would come to scavenge on the remaining carcasses.

At Lake Ilo, people made points with Folsom technology. A variety of tools and points found at Lake Ilo indicate that people stayed there long enough to replenish their toolkits.

Some of the animals killed were young calves, born the previous spring. By examining the stage of development of the calves' preserved teeth, archaeologists have determined that the hunt took place in early or mid-winter. It would have been cold and snow might have covered the ground. The hunting party made at least one fire. It is likely that they stayed long enough to eat a couple of meals, or perhaps it was a very cold day and they needed to warm themselves from time to time.

This Agate Basin point broke sometime before the two pieces were found by an archaeologist. The light-colored piece was exposed to weathering; the dark piece was buried. Archaeologists were able to put the pieces together by matching the edges at the breaking point.

While some members of the hunting party processed meat and prepared it for transport, others recovered projectile points from the carcasses and repaired them. Many of the points they brought with them on the hunt had been previously refurbished. The technology used by the people who hunted at Beacon Island identifies them as part of the Agate Basin culture. The people who knapped the long, slender (unfluted) Agate Basin points were careful to conserve and reuse their tools and weapons whenever possible. Tool workers sharpened and reshaped the recovered points. They could also rework broken points into another type of tool, perhaps a scraper or a knife. It seems likely that the Agate Basin point was designed so each piece could serve at least two purposes with refurbishing. The knappers also used up a few pieces of Knife River flint to make new tools while they waited for the

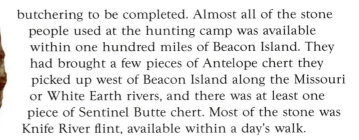

People of the Agate Basin culture reused tools or weapons that had become dull or broken with use. This tool, once a projectile point, was resharpened for secondary use.

butchering to be completed. Almost all of the stone people used at the hunting camp was available within one hundred miles of Beacon Island. They had brought a few pieces of Antelope chert they picked up west of Beacon Island along the Missouri or White Earth rivers, and there was at least one piece of Sentinel Butte chert. Most of the stone was Knife River flint, available within a day's walk.

This local stone used at Beacon Island tells us that this group of people had not simply wandered into this spot. They were very familiar with the available local resources, and even though they took advantage of occasional finds of chert or other suitable materials, they knew the value of good-quality Knife River flint and preferred it for their toolkit. It is not possible to say that this group always lived in this area, but they certainly knew the region well, and probably chose their winter camp because of the resources they could reliably locate here including Knife River flint and bison.

Even though this group might have been "locals," they had contact with other groups who left archaeological evidence of their presence in Wyoming, South Dakota, and Colorado. Whether this contact was regular or periodic, we can't be sure, but the people made similar tools and shared other cultural elements. Wherever people of the Agate Basin culture lived, they typically killed large numbers of bison, removed the upper limbs to transport to camp, and extracted marrow from the long bones. They all retrieved used or damaged stone tools and reworked them into useful tools.

The evidence at Beacon Island indicates that it was a place of work, but there are a few interesting bits of evidence that reveal more about their society. Three bone beads were found among the bits of bison bone and stone tools. It is not possible to know who wore a string of beads at the hunting camp, but it does suggest that this group of people lived in a society that valued personal decoration and had leisure time to pursue personal pleasures.

There were also some lumps of red ochre (hematite) and yellow ochre (limonite) and a few other pigments in white, pink, and orange. These pigments suggest that the people may have performed rituals before or after the hunt. It is possible that a person who held a position of spiritual leadership had accompanied the hunters.

Among the Agate Basin points and tools found at the site were two tools related to other cultural traditions. At least one Folsom point and one Goshen point were found at the site. The Folsom point was probably not used by the Beacon Island hunters. It may have been dropped at the site at another time. However, the Goshen point was used by Beacon Island hunters. Archaeologists have considered several possible conclusions from these two points. The first is that people who made Goshen tools lived at the same time as the people who made Agate Basin tools. It is very possible that some groups or individuals found the older point style useful and did not give it up in favor of the newer styles. Or, the different styles of points might suggest the co-existence of different cultural groups in the Plains region at the same time, much like American Indian tribes of the much-later historic period. Another idea is that the Agate Basin people who left Goshen points at their hunting camp had found those points lying around at another place they had visited. They picked them up, and being expert recyclers, made use of them.

Though Beacon Island was a hunting site, someone brought bone beads to the site. The beads were rounded and polished after the hole was drilled in the center.

Throughout the six thousand years of Paleoindian occupation of North Dakota, people moved in and out of the region, picking up stone, and finding places to camp where food, water, and shelter were abundant. There is evidence that Paleoindians camped as far east as the shores of the Red River and north along the Mouse River. It was a time of continuing change in lifestyle. The evidence found at places like Beacon Island and Bobtail Wolf indicates that people adapted to changing climate and consequent changes in animal and plant habitats, and they were probably part of increasing human populations on the Northern Great Plains. They developed new technologies and passed their knowledge on to younger generations and exchanged knowledge with other groups of people. They lived in societies that organized various activities into appropriate spaces, and perhaps assigned specific tasks according to gender and age as well. They planned their economies around seasonal needs and opportunities and graced events with spiritual rituals. They were skilled manufacturers of stone tools and kept a close eye on their resources in order to reduce the cost of production and maximize the use-life of their tools. Paleoindians were well prepared to adapt when new ideas about making and using tools and spiritual practices and beliefs flooded the grasslands of the Northern Great Plains.

Illustration by Greg Harlin—Wood Ronsaville Harlin, Inc.

At Beacon Island, people set up a small camp where they processed twenty-nine bison carcasses. They took large portions of the carcasses back to their main camp. This painting illustrates activities and the landscape discovered from artifacts and ecofacts recovered during the archaeological excavation at Beacon Island.

PALEOINDIAN PERIOD TIMELINE
12,000 TO 5500 BC

BC (RC Years Ago)	NORTH DAKOTA	NORTH AMERICA	WORLD
		— Corn cultivation, Mexico	
5850 BC (7,000 BP)	— Altithermal Period		— Pre-Dynastic, Egypt
6900 BC (8,000 BP)		— Modoc Rockshelter, IL	— Rice cultivation, China
8150 BC (9,000 BP)		— Atlatl, widespread adoption	
	— Beacon Island	— Agate Basin, WY	— Early Neolithic Era, Egypt
9500 BC (10,000 BP)	— Lake Ilo	— Folsom, NM	— Saharan rock art, Africa
11,000 BC (11,000 BP)	— Last glacial ice melts in North Dakota — Beach Cache	— Clovis, NM	— Monte Verde, Chile
12,000 BC (12,000 BP)			
13,600 BC (13,000 BP)			
14,000 BC (14,000 BP)		— Meadowcroft Rockshelter, PA	— Domesticated dogs, Russia
16,000 BC (15,000 BP)			
17,100 BC (16,000 BP)			
18,200 BC (17,000 BP)			— Lascaux Cave paintings, France
19,400 BC (18,000 BP)			
20,500 BC (19,000 BP)			
21,700 BC (20,000 BP)		— Bering Strait migration	

This timeline is based on published radiocarbon dates. The dates are listed as radiocarbon years before present (AD 1950) and BC / AD. The radiocarbon dates are not calibrated. The average calibrated date for Beacon Island is approximately 12,300 BP and for the Beach Cache 13,500 BP. Radiocarbon dates that are not calibrated become progressively too young with age; 5000 14C years is about 5700 calendar years, 11,000 14C years is about 13,000 calendar years, and 20,000 14C years is almost 24,000 calendar years.

Archaeological Method, Preservation and Documentation

When archaeologists examine a site, they use a variety of accepted practices and technologies in order to document the entire site, to preserve objects, and to gather data for analysis. Archaeologists, like other scientists, utilize technology along with documentation and analysis to learn more about the past.

For decades, the most common method of examining a buried archaeological site was to excavate or dig carefully into the ground with hand tools such as a shovel or a trowel. Prior to excavation, the site must be prepared with a grid pattern of square meter units so that every removed artifact is associated with a very specific location including the depth. This systematic documentation of location is known to archaeologists as provenience. Careful excavation prevents objects from becoming scattered due to careless digging; documentation of the excavation provides context for the object.

Dirt removed during excavations is carefully sifted through a fine screen to remove fragments of stone, bone, ceramics or other objects. Archaeologists often set up a wash station on site where excavated dirt is washed over a fine screen. Objects that did not wash through the screen are retained, labeled, and later processed and analyzed in a laboratory.

Though digging is still an important method for recovering archaeological data, archaeologists conduct less extensive excavations today. Excavation and analysis are expensive and very time-consuming. However, if a site has been uncovered by construction or some other disturbance, excavation may be the best and fastest way to examine the site and retrieve and preserve the artifacts.

Recent additions to the archaeologist's toolkit allow archaeologists to examine sites before excavating. These remote sensing technologies are magnetometry, ground penetrating radar, and LiDAR (Light Detection and Ranging). Magnetometry uses a device which measures variations in the magnetic properties of buried materials. The device records data that is processed and is reconfigured into images which appear on a computer screen. Magnetometry identifies features like fortification ditches, fire hearths, storage pits, roads, metals, and other structures or materials. Using this method, archaeologists in North Dakota learned that Double Ditch Village along the Missouri River just north of Bismarck actually had four fortification ditches two of which were previously unknown.

Human activity usually leaves some sort of mark or imprint on the landscape. Structural shapes, post molds, fire hearths, fortification ditches, and waste middens change the chemical properties and physical components of what was once the earth's surface. Ground penetrating radar is a technique which maps those changes on the sub-surface level without excavating the site. Ground penetrating radar can also determine the depth of the objects or anomalies of interest.

LiDAR creates 3-dimensional surface models or contour maps using an airborne laser scanner integrated with GPS (global positioning system). Brush, trees, and recent modifications to the landscape do not prevent the laser scanner from "seeing" details below the surface which might be invisible on the surface, yet of interest to an archaeologist.

Once objects are retrieved from a site and labeled, carefully preserved, and fully documented, an archaeologist may select an object for radiocarbon dating. Radiocarbon dating is applied only to objects that were living organisms sometime in the past 50,000 years. Stone, metal, and ceramic pottery were never alive so they cannot be carbon-dated, although biological residues on these objects may be. Radiocarbon dates reveal when the material was alive, not when it was used or for how long it was used. So, if a log was used to build a house and was later carbon-dated, we would learn when the tree died, but not necessarily when the house was built. Radiocarbon techniques date objects with a degree of certainty when used in conjunction with all of the information (context) available about the object including the provenience.

The radiocarbon dating technique involves measuring the amount of radioactive carbon-14 in the object. This isotope is available in the atmosphere and becomes part of a plant through photosynthesis—a natural and continuous process of living plants. Animals absorb carbon-14 from the plants they eat or, in the case of strict carnivores, from the flesh of the plant-eating animals they consume. When an animal or plant dies, its radioactive carbon content begins to decay at a known rate. Carbon-14 has a measurable half-life of 5,730 years. By the time the fossil or object is between 40,000 and 50,000 years old, the carbon-14 has been reduced to an unmeasurable amount.

Of course, there are problems associated with carbon dating. The sample may be contaminated with organic materials of a different age, or the material was created at a time when the radiocarbon concentration in the atmosphere was significantly different from its usual amount. It is also important to remember that radiocarbon dates are not the same as calendar dates. The value determined by carbon dating must be calibrated via a complex formula into calendar dates. The radiocarbon date is one of many pieces of data, including a controlled context, used in determining the age of an object or the dates of human occupation of a site.

These tools have vastly improved the ways in which archaeologists locate potential sites and isolate the most productive or relevant areas on a site for excavation. Modern technology, along with traditional excavation, have added a great deal to our understanding of ancient communities on the Northern Great Plains.

Archaeologists producing a detailed map at the Lynch Knife River Flint Quarries.

A magnetic survey and resistivity survey collected data that give a glimpse of what features may be beneath the surface prior to excavation.

Even the tiniest pieces of bone or stone are captured when dirt from the excavation units is washed through the fine window screen. Drying racks are to the left.

Prior to excavation, researchers establish a grid in one meter intervals using string. Each item found in the site is linked to its grid location.

The results of the magnetic survey at Double Ditch Indian Village State Historic Site. This guided locations of excavation units.

The anaylsis and report writing take substantially more time than fieldwork.

CHAPTER 2

GREAT INNOVATIONS

The Plains Archaic Era
5500 BC to 400 BC

At that time the people used dogs, for horses had not come yet.

Dadagua ita waaiigigh
wado ́ó mashuga wadeds,
iidzuwashga hidaagadza hiitadz.

– Bear's Arm, Hidatsa

Illustration by David Christy

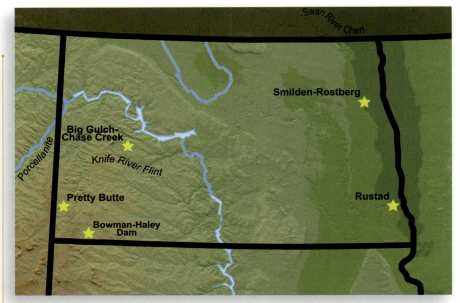

MAP 2.1. Important Archaic era sites in North Dakota.

Near the end of the Paleoindian cultural period, the climate and weather on the Northern Great Plains underwent a significant change. The Altithermal climate shift brought warmer, drier summers to the American West. Though scientists debate many effects of the Altithermal, it is thought to have had an impact on the Northern Great Plains from about 6000 to 3000 BC. During this time, North Dakota may have become so arid in the summer that Devils Lake dried up and the northern conifer forests in Canada retreated farther to the north. Though people still lived in the region or visited periodically, the population may have dropped as resources dependent on adequate rainfall, such as plants, animals, and lakes, responded to the stress of the warmer climate.

The Altithermal episode is partly responsible for the development of a new cultural period archaeologists identify as the Plains Archaic. The Early Plains Archaic is generally dated to about 5500 BC. Around this time, the people who lived here adjusted their lifeways to meet changing conditions.

It is primarily attendant changes in technologies and tools that mark the boundaries of the Plains Archaic cultural period. Gone are the beautifully crafted projectile points of the Paleoindian period. They are replaced by Archaic points that were notched on the sides, corners, or at the base

Archaic projectile points were not as skillfully made as Paleoindian points. Hunters securely hafted a point to the foreshaft of a dart with sinew.

28 | TRACES ▶ EARLY PEOPLES OF NORTH DAKOTA

and not as skillfully prepared as Clovis or Folsom points. However, the useful atlatl (*AT lat ill*), a handy spear-throwing device that added power to the throwing arm of Paleoindian hunters, was modified and improved by hunters of the Late Plains Archaic.

Bison remained the most important source of protein in human diets, but other foods included several species of large game and many small animals, too. There is evidence that plants, including leaves, roots, berries, and seeds, became more important to people during the Plains Archaic era than to earlier Paleoindians. People also used plant fibers to weave mats and bowls for personal comfort in their homes and for plant gathering and storage. People adopted clever and innovative new ways to cook food to accommodate the changes in their diet.

The Plains Archaic cultural period, however, presents a quandary or puzzle for archaeologists; there is little evidence to tell us about how the people of this time period lived in North Dakota. Some archaeologists hold a theory that the dry climate drove people (and the bison herds) out of the area and to places where the climate could better support the population. This theory, called the Altithermal Cultural Hiatus, has been vigorously debated, and many archaeologists disagree with it. However, many of these same archaeologists agree that bison herds were probably smaller or more scattered and that groups of people were likely to have been somewhat isolated from other groups. On both sides of the debate, archaeologists agree that people had to be innovative in order to adapt and thrive under the difficult conditions of the Altithermal.

The Rustad site is one of the earliest of the known Early Archaic sites in North Dakota. It is located in Richland County along the banks of the Sheyenne River, which provided a wooded setting for a relatively large camp of occupants. Because this site provided many necessary resources, it was used by different cultures over thousands of years. However, the Early Archaic material dominates the archaeological findings discussed here. From the remaining projectile points, bones, and features of human occupation, we learn something about life in the Early Archaic period.

Around 6100 BC (a little earlier than most Early Archaic sites), people made camp here in the summer months. Evidence suggests there were dozens of people comprising about twenty families. It is likely they did not stay here long, perhaps just a week or for part of the summer hunting season. They may have returned in winter for a short time.

Bison bison
Biology, Behavior, Ecology

Bison, often called buffalo, are native to North America. Ancient bison species include *B. latifrons*, *B. occidentalis*, and *B. antiquus*. These species appeared in succession, each a little smaller than the previous. Today, the American bison (*B. bison*) is smaller than its ancestors, but is still a formidable presence on the open grasslands. It is large (perhaps six feet high at the shoulder, up to two thousand pounds), horned, fast (up to thirty-five miles per hour), aggressive, and nomadic. Bison are ruminants who eat primarily grasses, and eat shrubs or lichen when grasses aren't available. When grass is buried in deep snow and unavailable to cattle and horses, bison use their immense, shaggy heads to clear away the snow. Their heavy coats keep them warm, and their habit of facing into the wind helps them withstand winter storms on the Great Plains.

Though bison do not see well, their size, aggressiveness, and senses of smell and hearing protect them. They can pick up scent on the wind as far as two miles away and hear predators moving through the grass. If the scent brings danger, the

(*Continued on next page*)

Bison were important game animals for every culture that lived on the Northern Great Plains. Bison may have become scarcer during the hot dry years of the Altithermal.

Bison bison
Biology, Behavior, Ecology
(Cont'd from page 21)

bulls raise their tails, and bellow a warning that can be heard three miles away. A bison bull attacks an aggressor with his head held low to shove up against the opponent; he then moves to the side to gore the opponent.

Though bison were once found nearly all over the continent, they thrived and multiplied in the prairies and plains. Estimates of the pre-1492 population of bison vary considerably, but a stable population of about twenty to thirty million is reasonable.

In the wild, breeding takes place in mid- to late summer. During the breeding season, bulls fight one another, but gently court females (cows). Cows select a mate, but not necessarily the largest or most aggressive male in the herd. The gestation period is about nine and one-half months. Typically, a single calf is born in March or April and is ready to stand and walk within minutes. The cow shelters and nurses her calf for six to nine months. A bison calf born in the wild might live about ten years.

Wild bison herds were deeply connected to Great Plains ecology. As they roamed in search of water and grass, they sought prairie dog towns where they rolled in the dusty, barren ground. Grasses leveled by grazing bison let prairie dogs see approaching predators. Water accumulated in bison wallows allowing water-loving sedges (*Carex spp*) to grow. Where bison grazed, both plains animals and plants diversified and thrived.

People occupied the Rustad site long enough to put up some sort of structure that seems to have been a semicircular wall large enough to provide shelter. A fire hearth was built within the semicircle and debris accumulated a few feet to one side, marking an area that might have been a portion of the wall. The shelter is small, about six and one-half feet (two meters) in diameter.

It appears that the people who occupied this camp spent most of their time hunting bison and processing their prey. The hunters killed bison somewhere else, probably not too far away, and brought the meat back to the camp to be cut into thin strips for cooking or drying. In addition to the meat, the people cracked the long bones from the bison carcass to remove the fatty marrow, a good source of calories and nutrition. The remains of eighteen bison, mostly mature animals, were found at the site. The bones indicate that the hunters had a preference for cows rather than bulls. Studies reveal that these bison were either *B. antiquus* or *B. occidentalis* species. Some scientists who specialize in faunal (animal) research believe *B. occidentalis* may have been less inclined to form large herds than modern bison and more difficult to maneuver into corrals, or pounds, for killing. Because of this, the hunters may not have killed a lot of animals in a single hunt, but they were very efficient at butchering, maximizing the harvest of meat and other parts of the carcass for the benefit of the community.

Once in a while, people caught and ate, or otherwise used, small animals such as skunks, rabbits, beavers, muskrats, and turtles. They also ate fish and freshwater mussels from the river, but the largest part of their diet seems to have been bison.

Dog or other types of canid bones were found at the Rustad camp. It is probable that dogs were companions as well as working dogs that transported bison meat, tools, or household goods. Some of the bison bones found in the camp had been gnawed by dogs. Archaeologists have determined from the size of the canid bones that some of these dogs were large enough to carry a pack weighing forty pounds. Though it is difficult to tell from the bones alone whether the animals were dogs or wolf hybrids, the gnawed bones and the usefulness of canines make it likely these were dogs kept for domestic purposes.

Dogs became essential to Archaic era families for several purposes, including transporting goods. *Illustration by David Christy*

The stone tools at this site indicate that bison hides were processed and perhaps made into articles such as tent covers or clothing. They (probably women) used stone or bone scrapers to clean and soften hides and pierced holes into thick tanned or untanned hides (rawhide) with sharpened stone or bone awls. It is possible they also used the soft skins of small animals in making garments. The range of activities suggests that entire families, not just hunters, lived and worked at this camp along the Sheyenne River for a while.

Scrapers and bone awls were used in hide working.

The lithics, or stones that had undergone a manufacturing process, retrieved from the Rustad site indicate that occupants made a full range of tools from start to finish at this camp. The assemblage includes many broken projectile points, and bifacial (sharpened on both sides) tools that had been broken during manufacture. In addition, hide-scrapers, spokeshaves, and several awls or piercing tools made of stone or other material were found at the site. Most of these tools were made from Swan River chert, a poor-quality stone for knapping commonly found in eastern North Dakota and southern Manitoba. Very few tools found at the Rustad site were made from Knife River flint.

Unlike the Paleoindian cultures that preceded them, the people who made camp at the Rustad site in the Early Plains Archaic era made notched projectile points. The notches near the base on each side were used to securely haft (attach) the point to the wooden shaft. The predominant style at Rustad has been classified as Logan Creek/Mummy Cave (or perhaps Simonsen side-notched). These styles were commonly produced on the Northern and Northeastern Great Plains and are named for important Plains Archaic sites in Nebraska and Wyoming respectively.

The Logan Creek points found at Rustad are less than one and one-half inches long and less than one-quarter inch thick. They were manufactured as small points, not refurbished from larger points. These points are small enough that they might be mistaken for arrow points of a later era, but there is no evidence that the bow and arrow were known or used at this time. These points were probably made for use with darts meant to be hurled toward a target with the aid of an atlatl. It is possible Archaic hunters fletched their darts with feathers inserted into the far end of the shaft. A fletched dart with a small point launched with an atlatl was a lethal weapon that could be aimed accurately and thrown with power as far as one hundred yards away. The small points effectively penetrated the thick bison coat and hide. Early Archaic hunters also likely used spears to finish off a wounded animal. The Early Archaic hunters at the Rustad camp were capable of using more than one weapon system to hunt and kill multiple species of animals.

scraper   spokeshave

At the Rustad site, hunters knapped small projectile points in the Logan Creek/Mummy Cave style. Scrapers and spokeshaves were also part of their toolkit.

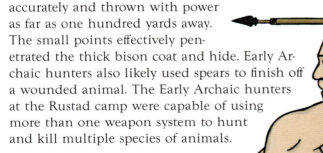

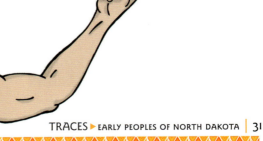

TRACES ▶ EARLY PEOPLES OF NORTH DAKOTA 31

During a time of warm and dry climatic conditions at the camp now known as Smilden-Rostberg, a few families killed and processed four bison. *Museum Division, SHSND*

There is great diversity in the style, quality, and lithic materials of points made during the Archaic period.

These Pretty Butte projectile points were knapped in the parallel-oblique flaked lanceolate style typical of the Paleoindian era.

The Rustad camp tells us quite a bit about the Early Archaic cultural tradition in North Dakota, but it also raises important questions. The people at Rustad appear to have hunted mostly bison; bison bones comprise eighty percent of the animal bones found at the site. Certainly, bison were attracted to shelter, food, and water along the Sheyenne River, making it a good spot for a short-term camp of large game hunters. Does the high percentage of bison bones mean that herds were large and easily found? Did the people of Rustad have the luxury of easy access to bison and, therefore, not have to kill more than a few animals at a time? Or, had the drought of the Altithermal diminished the herds and the Rustad hunters killed as many as possible of the few bison they found near their camp? Did the people have to move camp frequently to keep up with scarce herds or to avoid other groups of people who were hungry enough to challenge their command of this location?

Another Early Archaic site is located near present-day Larimore (Grand Forks County), on the Turtle River. This site, known today as Smilden-Rostberg, has revealed the activities of a group of hunters who butchered four bison one mid-winter day about 3844 BC. At this camp, a few people, perhaps one or two families, sought small herds or individual game animals. They used side-notched and corner-notched dart points of varying sizes, similar to those found at Rustad. Only one of the nine points was made of Knife River flint, and flaking debris indicates they worked on some of their tools while butchering the four bison. The hunters had their dogs with them and apparently tied them up a few feet away from where they were butchering and gave them some bones to gnaw. The ring of dog-chewed bones is just out of reach of the cluster of butchered bison bones. Archaeologists found the skulls of the slaughtered bison arranged neatly, upright, and within three feet of one another. The arrangement appears to have been deliberate. However, we do not know whether the arrangement of the skulls was meaningful, perhaps spiritual in nature.

It is striking that the lithic materials at Rustad and Smilden-Rostberg indicate very little use of Knife River flint. The stone knappers seem to have been content with Swan River chert and other local stones, even though those stones were inferior to Knife River flint. The work of the knappers no longer had the beautifully refined qualities of those who made Clovis or Folsom points several thousand years earlier. The points were a little lopsided and the edges were jagged, not smooth and sharp. Archaeologists conclude from this evidence that Early Archaic people did not move about as often or travel as far as earlier residents of the Northern Plains had. They did not routinely travel the couple hundred miles west to the Knife River flint quarries in present-day Dunn County to mine superior quality flint. They appear more isolated, and had somehow lost some of the flintknapping skills of the Folsom era people who preceded them.

An interesting site, located near Pretty Butte in the badlands northwest of Marmarth, offers another puzzle to archaeologists. Charcoal found in a hearth at the Pretty Butte site has been dated to 3478 BC, which places it well within the Early Archaic cultural period. This was probably a small camp where the people stayed for a while to refurbish their tool kits, cook meals, and take care of their needs. It is not known if the people hunted while camped there, because there is no evidence of killing or butchering at the site. The significance of the Pretty Butte site is in the type of projectile points found here.

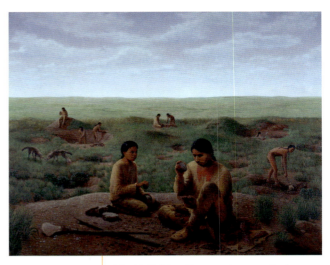

The Knife River flint quarries were the best source of good quality stone in the Northern Great Plains. *Museum Division, SHSND*

The points made and used at Pretty Butte do not fit the usual cultural classification of this time period. They were knapped in a style archaeologists call Parallel Oblique—an unnotched, lanceolate (leaf-shaped) point usually associated with the Late Paleoindian tradition on the Northern Plains. However, like Early Archaic groups, the people at Pretty Butte knapped tools from several types of stone such as silicified wood and chalcedony that could be found nearby. Only two tools found at the site were crafted from Knife River flint. Though the Knife River flint quarry was less than 125 miles northeast of Pretty Butte, the people apparently did not use this resource. It is possible, of course, that they were planning to go to the quarries soon. On the other hand, perhaps they were not familiar with the quarries, or they did not need the finer knapping materials. They may have been content to live in a narrower geographic range and use the resources available, but it is also possible they feared it was not safe to travel to the quarries.

Aerial view of the Lynch Knife River Flint Quarries. These small depressions on the landscape indicate where people mined flint over thousands of years.

Two of the four points found at Pretty Butte were well made with uniform flaking patterns reflecting techniques employed by Paleoindian point knappers. Conversely, the other two lanceolate points were not well made; an archaeologist described the knapper's work as "haphazard." So, two of the points found at the site were of a style and technique associated with cultures of a much earlier time, but two of the points reflect the less-skilled knapping abilities of other Early Archaic era stoneworkers.

Climate Change

The region of North America that North Dakota now occupies has a dynamic climate history. Humans arrived in North Dakota as the last glaciers were retreating to the north and east. About 9,000 years ago, a climate trend known as the Hypsithermal warmed much of North America. The generally dry Hypsithermal summers led to expansion of the grasslands, but also to drought and soil erosion. Wind attacked dry soils to create the sand dunes of the Souris, Pembina and Sheyenne river deltas. However, periods of high moisture also filled Devils Lake, sometimes to overflowing levels, only to be followed by dry spells and a dry lake bed.

The Hypsithermal came to an end about 2,000 years ago. Temperatures stabilized, though extremes of temperatures and moisture conditions appeared irregularly. A notable cooling trend, called the Little Ice Age, affected conditions on the Northern Great Plains (and the rest of the northern hemisphere) from 1550 to 1850. During this three-hundred-year period, temperatures sometimes cooled enough to limit the growing season for both wild and domesticated plants. Scientists identify periods of drought and rainfall by measuring the width of tree rings, a science known as dendrochronology. While this method is very reliable, the grasslands climate, regular prairie fires, and use of trees for housing and fuel, limits the scope of dendrochronology in

(Continued on next page)

  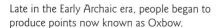

Late in the Early Archaic era, people began to produce points now known as Oxbow.

This site highlights the difficult task facing archaeologists who must reconcile absolute dates (such as radiocarbon dates) with relative dates derived from a cluster of projectile points that have diagnostic attributes or knapping styles of a particular time period. The dates determined by radiocarbon assays on the remains of the camp fire at Pretty Butte have been carefully studied and analyzed, and archaeologists are fairly certain the date of 3478 BC determined for this site is accurate, give or take one hundred years or so. This means the Pretty Butte site departs from the data collected at other Early Archaic and Late Paleoindian sites; it does not clearly fall into either cultural period, though it is often called a Paleoindian site. How should outliers like Pretty Butte be analyzed and explained?

If we assume the Pretty Butte group experienced life in much the same way that modern people do, we might direct the questions toward familiar possibilities. Was this group part of a culture under stress from warfare or disease? Perhaps their language or spiritual views made them incompatible with other regional groups. Or, was this a "remnant culture" or refugium of hunters and gatherers who continued to make lanceolate points long after others had abandoned the tradition? Is it possible they had been isolated for a long time and were content with the tools and technologies they had? It could be that new ideas in technology, such as the change in point styles from Late Paleoindian lanceolate to Early Archaic small, notched, spread more slowly than once thought. We don't know the answers to these important questions, but someday archaeologists may uncover more evidence at other sites that will offer a new perspective on Pretty Butte and the people who lived there. The questions raised at the Pretty Butte site remind us that culture, as adaptation, is a term subject to redefinition by small, challenging exceptions.

Late in the Early Archaic period, people manufactured points in a style now known as Oxbow. The last years of the Early Archaic period are defined by the Oxbow projectile point, which was in use from approximately 3300 to 2500 BC. The original Oxbow cultural discovery was at a place called Oxbow in the Souris River Basin in southern Saskatchewan. The point is distinctive, with notches and "ears" projecting downward from the base. It is seldom mistaken for other points. Oxbow points are more common in North Dakota than earlier Archaic points and have been found throughout the state. The remarkable trait of the Oxbow point is that it has been recovered at sites representing a variety of landscapes in the region. The people of the Archaic cultural tradition used the point on the plains, in the Canadian forests to the north, and in the prairie-forest ecotone where the vegetation transitions from grassy prairie to forest. The widespread use of the Oxbow point suggests the people of the Early Archaic tradition had extensive knowledge of the habitat and behavior of a wide variety of game animals and were able to adapt their hunting skills to bison, moose, elk, and caribou, as well as small game. Another climate shift coincided with cultural changes to define the Middle Plains Archaic period (2800 to 1000 BC). The long, periodic droughts of the Altithermal episode gave way to cooler temperatures and higher levels of moisture of the Sub-Boreal climate episode. The climate shift brought about greater variety and abundance in vegetation on the Northern Great Plains. Though the climate shifts and their impact on the Great Plains have been vigorously debated by archaeologists, evidence suggests the slightly cooler, wetter climate brought about an increase in both the human and bison populations in the region that is now North Dakota. Indeed, the archaeological sites associated with the Middle Plains Archaic tradition outnumber those of the Early Plains Archaic in North Dakota.

The major cultural tradition of this time period is called the McKean Complex after the McKean lanceolate points widely used in this region. McKean-style projectile points replaced Oxbow points in North Dakota. However, to the north, in Saskatchewan and Manitoba, people continued to use Oxbow points for many more years. Concurrent production and use of different types of projectile points by different groups of people, and even within one group, is common throughout the Archaic period.

One day, during the Middle Plains Archaic era, on a high bluff overlooking a tributary of Chase Creek, some people made a camp about four miles from the Little Missouri River and five miles from the Killdeer Mountains. This location is now called the Big Gulch–Chase Creek site. These steep gullies are in the heart of the rough country of the badlands in western North Dakota. It was a good place for elk and deer to find winter shelter and food.

The people who occupied Big Gulch–Chase Creek produced McKean-style projectile points from Knife River flint, chalcedony, porcellanite, and other local stones. McKean points are lanceolate (leaf-shaped) with a wide midsection, narrowing sharply to the tip. They have a deeply concave (in-curved) base. Broken and discarded pieces of debitage (the portions of stone removed) and four hammerstones indicate that knappers were working stone into tools from start to finish. More than eighty percent of the lithic materials were manufactured from Knife River flint, which could be found within two miles of the bluff.

In the Middle Archaic era, hunters made projectile points archaeologists call McKean.

CLIMATE CHANGE
(Cont'd)

North Dakota. However, by combining available tree ring data with historical accounts, scientists are able to fill in the climate history of North Dakota.

Archaeologists are interested in climate change because periods of erosion have nearly erased evidence of human occupation. Wind-drifted soil can obscure structures and fill depressions. High water levels on riverbanks and lakeshores wash away the remains of campsites. On the other hand, the accumulation, or layering, of certain soil types is associated with particular geologic events and can help to determine the date of an archaeological site.

Archaeologists use climate change data to assess movements of ancient cultures. Drought would signal a period of migration to wetter locations, or even out of the region altogether. Extreme cold would have a similar effect. Human (and animal) populations of the Northern Great Plains fluctuated in response to climatic conditions, but climate also stimulated innovative technologies that made life comfortable in spite of the climate.

The badlands provided excellent place for people to hunt elk, deer, and bison and find fruit-bearing shrubs. The Big Gulch-Chase Creek site is located in the badlands. Illustration by *David Christy*

An antler billet is used to strike off flakes during the initial shaping of this biface. The finer finishing is completed utilizing a pressure flaker.

The process of manufacturing a projectile point is divided into several steps. The first blows were meant to form an edge all the way around a blank (stone that has been worked into the beginning stages of a point, but not completed). These strikes provided the first test of the stone's quality and tested the skill of the knapper in working with that type of stone. Flaws in the stone would be revealed when the hammer struck them and the stone shattered. The knapper had to apply great force to remove a desired portion of stone (flake) from the blank. Every blow carried the risk of an unwanted fracture. If the knapper did not control the blows carefully, the stone fractured unintentionally. Very small pieces (debitage) were discarded. However, once the knapper had achieved a relatively well-shaped point, the remaining stages of the process were less likely to result in a pile of useless and discarded flakes.

On the other hand, being practical producers of tools, the knappers might have chosen to produce a biface with a sharp edge to be used as a cutting tool, rather than finishing it into a projectile point. Used and broken cutting tools make up a portion of the broken bifaces found at Big Gulch.

Among the flakes recovered at Big Gulch–Chase Creek are three pieces of obsidian and a few other exotic stones not typically found in this region. It is possible that some of these were found in small quantities locally, but obsidian typically derives from the Rocky Mountains near Yellowstone. These exotic stones suggest a couple of different possibilities. Either this group traveled more widely than peoples of the Early Archaic, or they were engaged in trade with more distant travelers. Either way, they seemed to have opportunities for broader contacts with other cultures and learned to use a variety of stone types to fashion the tools they needed.

American Indian women processed chokecherries with a grinding stone in the early 20th century much as did women of the Archaic era. *A2231*

Stone tools found at Big Gulch–Chase Creek reveal a busy camp. Hunters returned from a pursuit with weapons damaged by impact fractures, a common misfortune. Some weapons had broken points still hafted to dart shafts. To repair the weapons, they removed the broken points and then refitted the shaft with new points. The carcasses of the animals killed in the hunt were processed in camp with stone cutting tools and the hides were cleaned with stone scrapers. The toolkits of these badlands hunters also included four spokeshaves, three punches or splitting wedges, and a graver or grooving tool. With these tools they split wood or bone (using splitting wedges), and then shaved (using spokeshaves) and rounded lengths of these split pieces for use as dart shafts or atlatls.

Other work in the camp, perhaps the work of women, included scraping and perforating hides. These hides were probably made into clothing, containers, or shelter covers by punching holes into them with a sharply pointed awl and sewing pieces together. They also used tools to chop, shred, and pulp plants. They used a sharp stone knife to slice meat and plant foods, and a metate (meh TAH tay), also called a grinding stone, to grind seeds into digestible flours. It is very likely that food preparation was mostly the work of women, who not only processed plants and meat for meals but for winter storage as well.

Prickly pear cactus is found throughout western North Dakota. The pads are edible and juicy. *Courtesy of John and Mary Bluemle*

In the Middle Archaic period, people began to cook in new ways. They still used hearths built on the surface of the ground, but they also dug basin-shaped pits that they lined with rocks. The rocks, heated by fire, formed a kind of oven where they roasted their food. They also took fire-heated rocks from the pit and placed them in a water container—probably a bag made of animal hide or a tightly woven basket—to boil their food. This is called "hot rock cooking." The rocks were heated over and over until they cracked from the heat and were discarded. At Big Gulch–Chase Creek, the broken rocks were piled up away from the hearth.

This copper awl from the Boots site indicates that people living in North Dakota engaged in trade with peoples who had acquired trade goods from the Great Lakes region.

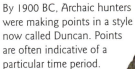

The camp at Big Gulch–Chase Creek was not unique. People of Middle Archaic cultures often hunted and camped on the ridges that dominate the landscape along the Little Missouri River, leaving bits and pieces of their lives as they moved from one camping spot to another. The ridges were ideal for access to water and large game. Fruit-bearing shrubs and other plants were available. Studies of the pollens remaining in these sites' soils indicate that people probably processed the fruit of prickly pear cactus (*Opuntia polycantha*). Archaeologists also found cattail (*Typha* species) pollen which is edible, and other parts of the plant can be used as food or fiber. Milkwort (*Polygala alba*) pollen has also been found at the camp sites. It may have had medicinal use as a treatment for earache.

By 1900 BC, Archaic hunters were making points in a style now called Duncan. Points are often indicative of a particular time period.

Along the ridges, knappers of the Middle Archaic period learned or developed a new style of stemmed projectile point that archaeologists call Duncan. Through trade, they acquired some copper tools including an awl found at a site now called Boots. The source of the copper is not known with certainty, but it probably was brought from a source near the Upper Great Lakes.

Pelican Lake points mark the beginning of the Late Plains Archaic era. The points are symmetrical and sharply pointed.

Hunters left Duncan points and at least one McKean point near a creek that feeds a branch of the Grand River in Bowman County in the southwestern corner of North Dakota. Today this is the site of the Bowman-Haley Dam, but long ago, the junction of the two streams was for several hundred years an appealing place to camp. About 1800 BC, the people who stayed here built a structure, perhaps a house or other type of shelter, that left a distinct depression in the ground. It was about ten feet in diameter and one-half foot deep. Archaeologists are not certain that these post molds indicate people built domestic shelters. Nevertheless, evidence is accumulating to suggest that by the Middle Archaic period people in this region had the means and the skills to construct temporary shelters.

Archaeologists identify a third period of the Plains Archaic period as the Late Plains Archaic (1000 to 400 BC). At this time on the Northern Great Plains, the Sub-Atlantic climate episode resulted in wetter summers and alternating episodes of warm and cool temperatures. The wetter climate may have led to an abundance of plants to support humans as well as the animals they hunted. This time period is identified with innovations in food preparation and hunting as well as a new style point called Pelican Lake that was typically medium-sized and triangular in shape with corner notches.

Chenopodium (goosefoot or lamb's quarters) is a common weed of North Dakota, but it was an important source of food for peoples of the Archaic era. *Courtesy, Tom Peters and NDSU Extension*

A number of Emmons County sites in south central North Dakota reveal additional information about the Late Plains Archaic period. The people who made camps in the Emmons County hills ate fish as well as bison, small mammals, and birds. They gathered the seeds of goosefoot (also called lamb's quarters or wild spinach; *Chenopodium* species) and ground them for use as food. People who came here to collect plants or hunt left stone circles at one of the Emmons County sites. It is not clear that the stone circles represent the rings of heavy stones used to weigh down the edges of tipis (conical, skin-covered structures), but they certainly represent a specific purpose in human activity.

A bannerstone or weight gave stability and force to the atlatl.

The atlatl had a hook on one end that stabilized the dart as the hunter prepared to throw it. Atlatl hooks could be made of bone as was this one.

Archaeologists have found broken long bones of large animals and fire-cracked rocks at the Emmons County sites. The long bones had to be broken to remove the nutritious bone marrow. The presence of fire-cracked rocks suggests that people who lived in this region about 1300 BC had the materials and technology necessary to extract marrow by boiling the broken bones. They heated stones and dropped them into a watertight hide container filled with water. The boiling water cooked the bones and released the fat from the marrow. The heated fat rose to the surface of the water and, when cooled, became a solid material that could be stored for later use. Earlier peoples probably removed marrow directly from the bone, but by the Late Plains Archaic period, people processed fat to use in preserving foods for long-term storage and in preparing high-calorie foods for winter.

Hunters of the Late Plains Archaic still used atlatls—as had Paleoindians before them—but they modified and improved the weapon by applying weights to increase their accuracy. The atlatl was a small piece of wood about two feet long. A hook carved from an antler was fitted at one end and a handle was applied at the opposite end. The hunter placed the end of a dart (without the stone point) into the hook. When the hunter launched the dart toward a target, he held onto the atlatl while the dart flew through the air with fifteen times more velocity and force than a dart could be thrown without the assistance of the atlatl. The extra weight of a bannerstone improved the stability of the weapon by balancing the weight of the dart. Bannerstones had a hole bored through the stone that were long, tubular, or wing-shaped. The bannerstone then slid over the shaft of the atlatl. Atlatl weights were tied on with sinew. Some were carved into beautiful shapes representing animals.

There are many elegant designs on these artifacts. Atlatl weights and bannerstones may also be a form of art with spiritual or aesthetic appeal.

It is very likely that cultural life of the Plains Archaic tradition in North Dakota was just as rich as elsewhere on the Northern Great Plains where dry caves or rock shelters have preserved much of the material culture of the Archaic era. At other locations, particularly Mummy Cave in Wyoming, archaeologists have found baskets and mats woven from lengths of cord spun from plant leaves and fibers. Archaeologists have not yet found similar artifacts at North Dakota sites, because conditions in North Dakota did not favor preservation of plant-based objects. However, people probably wove similar baskets and mats to use for gathering and storing plants, roots, and berries. Some weavers may have been skillful enough to fashion watertight baskets from plant fibers that could be used in boiling plants, bones, or meat. Before making a basket, the weaver had to prepare cordage from plant fibers by twisting fibers of yucca or milkweed together to form a rope, thread, or string. Cordage was also used in stitching pieces of hide together or to make a thong to tie a knife to the wrist or the waist, or perhaps to tie one's belongings to one's back—or better yet, to a dog's back. Some weavers or sewers may have made cordage from sinew taken from a bison or elk carcass, or mixed sinew with plant fibers to make long, strong cords.

Copper points

Though plants played an increasingly important role in Plains Archaic societies, archaeologists do not believe that people living on the Northern Plains cultivated domesticated plants at this time. However, increasing use and dependence on plants probably directed small groups of families to migrate to places where they could obtain necessary plants at the proper time of year.

Olivella shells

People of Archaic cultures made adornments such as beads or pendants from bone, shells, or copper. Shells (*Olivella* species) came from the Pacific Ocean, and copper came from the Great Lakes region. These exotic materials indicate trade took place over great distances. People may have traded Knife River flint or bison meat and hides for materials they

Hunters moved herds of bison across open land to a cliff. The animals stampeded over the cliff where they died or were severely injured. *Museum Division, SHSND*

could not find locally. Trade items were used to make decorative pieces, but it is possible beads and pendants had spiritual significance, too.

While bison hunting remained the most important economic activity for the people of the Plains Archaic period, they also used their deep knowledge of bison behavior to improve on existing hunting methods. The hunt had to be very well organized. People worked together to locate a herd and maneuver the animals into a situation and setting that allowed the hunters to kill as many animals as the community needed. A hunting method commonly referred to as a "buffalo jump" was used where cliffs or high, steep river banks were part of the landscape. Hunters drove a herd over the edge of the cliff where other hunters waited to kill the surviving animals. Though cliffs were not abundant in North Dakota, hunters found a few locations that served as jumps.

More often, Archaic hunters built a corral-like structure called a pound. This was made of log posts set into the ground and interwoven with branches and disguised with brush. The pound worked best in a landscape of rolling terrain with steep coulees. The breaks or broken landscape of the Missouri and Little Missouri Rivers and other deep-cut river valleys provided such a setting. Some of the people drove the animals along a path that terminated at the pound. The pound, properly placed and covered with brush or hides, could not be seen until the animals were entering the corral. Confused, the bison milled about as the hunters hiding in the brush used spears and darts to kill the animals.

Hunters would sometimes build a pound and corral animals to be killed.

When bison herds were scarce, people made use of other large game, smaller animals, birds, and fish. They fished with hooks of bone or gouges carved from wood. Corded netting also may have been used to trap fish. Archaic hunters and cooks adjusted their tasks to suit the environment.

The Plains Archaic period drew to a close about 400 BC as people of the Northern Great Plains once again adopted new technologies and beliefs. They did not give up older traditions, such as the Pelican Lake point, but melded new skills with old to improve their lives. They were influenced by ideas common among the people who lived in the forested river valleys east of the Great Plains, where Woodland cultures were already working clay into vessels and building mounds for burial of their dead. Indeed, to the south, in the Central Great Plains, people of the Late Archaic tradition were already using clay to make watertight vessels by the end of the Late Archaic era. It would not be long before the new ideas traveled trade routes to North Dakota.

Plains Archaic Period Timeline
5500 to 400 BC

BC/AD	NORTH DAKOTA	NORTH AMERICA	WORLD
AD 1		— Basketmaker II period in the Southwest — Hopewell Culture in Eastern North America	— Rise of Athens, Greece — Birth of Buddha — Nubian Kingdom rises, Sudan / Egypt — Polynesian settlements, Fiji / Samoa
1200 BC	— Pelican Lake Complex 1000-400 BC — Sub-Atlantic Climate 1000-400 BC	— Sunflower domesticated — Olmec Culture, Mesoamerica — Chenopodium domesticated	
2500 BC	— McKean Complex 2500-2000 BC — Duncan Complex 2000-1500 BC — Hanna Complex 1500-1000 BC — Sub-Boreal Climate 2800-1000 BC — Oxbow Complex 3300-2500 BC — Pretty Butte Site — Smilden-Rostberg Site	— Poverty Point occupation — Old Copper Culture	— Tin-bronze production in central Europe — Stonehenge, England 3000-2000 BC — Great Pyramid of Egypt is constructed
3800 BC			— Hieroglyphic script, Egypt
4900 BC			— Copper production in the Balkans
5850 BC		— Corn cultivation, Mexico	
	— Rustad Site		
6900 BC	— Altithermal Period 6900-2800 BC		— First agricultural settlement of Europe

Late Archaic 1000-400 BC
Middle Archaic 2800-1000 BC
Early Archaic 5500-2800 BC

TRACES ▸ EARLY PEOPLES OF NORTH DAKOTA

Legislation for Preservation

In 1906, President Theodore Roosevelt signed the Antiquities Act. This law, the first to acknowledge the significance of archaeological sites, requires federal agencies that manage public lands to preserve sites with historic, scientific, commemorative, and cultural value. During the previous decades, the American people had become aware that the vast expanse of land in the public domain was disappearing to settlement and development. The nation set out to preserve portions of that domain as places of spiritual renewal and important national resources. Consequently, Congress established national forests and national parks.

Individuals in both public and private positions, including professionals in the new field of archaeology, sought to protect sites on public lands that were endangered due to development or looting. Already many artifacts had been taken from sites on public lands by people involved in the commercial artifact trade. Under the American Antiquities Act, archaeological and historic sites can be managed and protected. Collections from archaeological sites and cultural resources are to be managed for scientific study as well as cultural interpretation for the public.

The Antiquities Act established the precedent of protecting the public's interest in archaeological sites. The law provides for qualified institutions or professionals to obtain permission to investigate sites which may include excavation and collection of artifacts that would advance knowledge of the cultural value of the site. The federal government cooperates with state, tribal, and local governments and agencies to enforce the law and manage archaeological sites.

In 1966, Congress passed another federal law to protect historic and archaeological sites. The National Historic Preservation Act provided for protection of historic sites, our nation's heritage, from development, particularly by federal agencies. Under this law, federal governmental agencies in partnership with state or tribal agencies may identify historic properties to protect. This law differs from the Antiquities Act of 1906 in that it monitors federal development, it applies to historic as well as archaeological sites, and it works at the community level. People have used the National Historic Preservation Act to transform their communities through historic preservation. Many communities continue to see social and economic benefits resulting from these preservation efforts.

Since the passage of the Historic Preservation Act and the establishment of the National Register of Historic Places, more than 89,000 sites have been listed nationally. These include privately- and publicly-owned properties, archaeological sites, and historic districts in villages, towns, and cities across the country. The law has led to more care in urban planning, preservation of important buildings and locations, and economic growth.

The law recognizes that the "spirit and direction of the Nation are founded upon and reflected in its historic heritage." With this statement, Congress asks all of us to hold onto and value continuing cultural activity and change in our communities. Furthermore, the law states that "historical and cultural foundations of the Nation should be preserved as a living part of our community life . . . in order to give a sense of orientation to the American people." As a living historic community, we draw from archaeology to understand the thousands of years of tradition, innovation, and resilience that shaped our country's past and continue to shape its future.

The National Historic Preservation Act enables recovery of important information that then can be presented to the public in multiple forms, including exhibits.

The Innovation Gallery: Early Peoples at the North Dakota Heritage Center and State Museum.

Tribal Historic Preservation Offices provide valuable advice regarding significance of archaeological sites.

When archaeological sites are going to be disturbed by developments archaeological excavations preserve information about the resource.

The Independence Congregational Mission Church and Cemetery is listed on the National Register of Historic Places for broad patterns in history. The US government relocated the graves and church imperiled by the construction of Garrison Dam.

Gail and Allan Lynch pursued the Lynch Knife River Flint Quarries registration as a National Historic Landmark.

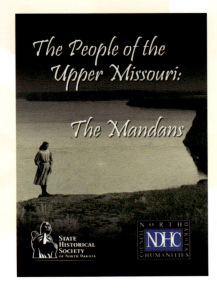

This film benefitted by combining Native American knowledge with results from excavations at multiple archaeological sites to provide a deeper understanding of the past.

Chapter 3

Influences from the East

Plains Woodland Cultures
400 BC to AD 1200

In making pottery one must mix certain clays with sand or grit produced by crushing certain stones long used around the fires.

Middaxa dibia hiddidug uugadagi adu dibia middá iiaxahaa mí habi adu tsíihe magília shaha adu dia iidíha.

– Hidatsa, origins of pottery, Alfred Bowers 1965

Illustration by Andrew Knudson

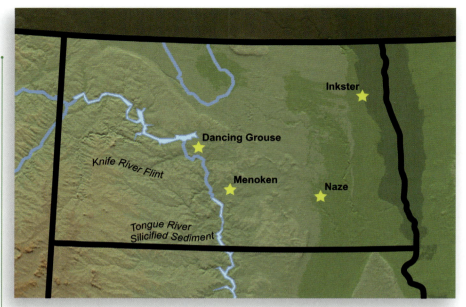

Map 3.1. Plains Woodland era sites and lithic resource areas in North Dakota.

By the first years of the Early Plains Woodland tradition, around 400 BC, people had occupied North Dakota for thousands of years. Geomorphic (landscape shape and features) and stratigraphic (layers of earth, stone, and/or artifacts) studies of archaeological sites show layers correlated with repeated human occupation over hundreds or even thousands of years. Sites near water, wood, plant, and animal resources attracted people time and again no matter what cultural traits and traditions they embraced. These were the good places to set up a home or hunting camp. The archaeological record does not tell us whether people came to these sites because their forebears—parents and grandparents—had, or because they simply sought out places with the resources that people always need. Nevertheless, the continuity of occupation reminds us that the people of a variety of cultures shared certain interests in meeting the needs of their communities.

The east-central part of North Dakota is characterized by rolling grasslands, small water holes, and rocky soil.

Plains Woodland cultures are subdivided into Early (400 to 100 BC), Middle (100 BC to AD 600) and Late Plains Woodland (AD 600 to 1700s). Each period had distinctive cultural characteristics that differentiated and shaped the social relations and economies of the groups of people living in the region. During these centuries, the Northern Great Plains, or Northeastern Plains as the region is known to archaeologists, had a climate very similar to our own during the time of the Plains Woodland cultures.

Researchers have described the climate of the Plains Woodland era as "mesic," meaning it was a moderately moist habitat. Residents of the time could expect adequate rainfall and relatively warm (for this latitude) temperatures. However, the rainfall was inadequate to support great forests. This region was dominated by grasslands on flat to rolling plains in the eastern two-thirds of the state. Along the western edge, the landscape was characterized by badlands where creeks and rivers separated rocky ridges. Though waterways supported riparian forests, this was not an area that could be described as typically "woodland."

The badlands environment has rocky hillsides cut away by erosion to deep coulees and grassy meadows. *Photo courtesy of Dave Nix*

In the grassland environment, the term Plains Woodland seems contradictory, but it describes the cultures of the people who lived on the Plains at this time. They drew on certain cultural traits and traditions that were common among the people who lived east and south of North Dakota, particularly in the well-watered and forested region that today encompasses Illinois, Indiana, Ohio, Iowa, and Minnesota. Woodland traits became part of the cultures of the people living in North Dakota either through the exchange of materials and ideas along trade networks or via the migration of eastern Woodland peoples onto the Plains.

Plains Woodland cultures left evidence of their occupation in North Dakota which archaeologists uncovered hundreds or thousands of years later. During the Plains Woodland era, the population of the region very likely increased, resulting in more opportunities for archaeologists to study these ancient cultures. In addition, time and weather have had less impact on Plains Woodland sites than on earlier sites, so there are some remarkable artifacts to tell the stories.

Artist's vision of the Naze village, an Early Plains Woodland site on the banks of the James River. The painting is based on archaeological evidence found at the site. *Illustration by Andrew Knudson*

Broken pieces of pottery, bone and stone tools, and animal bones provide clues to activities occurring at the Naze site.

Good luck for modern archaeologists, however, began as bad luck for a family who set up their household at the confluence of Beaver Creek and the James River in the southeast corner of Stutsman County. Their settlement, containing a domestic structure, possibly a house, is today known as the Naze (NAH zee) site after the family that presently owns that land. The structure was built using four pairs of bur oak posts set upright into holes in the ground and supported with firmly-packed clay daub. The wall covering of their house may have been made of hide, brush, or wide strips of bark. Archaeologists estimate that the structure enclosed a space that was probably about four to six meters (thirteen to twenty feet) in diameter. The building was large enough for a family to conduct its daily activities.

One day, between 550 and 410 BC, the house was consumed by fire and burned to the ground. The wall supports and wall coverings burned to ash, but the fire was hot enough to harden the clay at the base of the central support posts. A careful archaeological dig of about one percent of the site revealed much information about this family and their lifeways. We do not know the fate of the family, but their tools and other goods were left where they had been stored inside the house. The eight oak center posts burned down to charred stumps and fired clay. It was these charred posts and fired clay daub that archaeologists identified with magnetometry readings taken on the surface.

Modern potters study potsherds from the Naze site to replicate the original pot's size, shape, and decorative design.

Among the debris found at the site were fire-cracked rocks, bones, stone tools, and pieces of broken pottery (ceramic potsherds). The ceramics are very interesting because they point to one of the major cultural traits of the Plains Woodland period. For the first time on the Northern Plains, people were making and using fired clay vessels. Clay, or ceramic, pots made excellent containers for storing water and food, as well as for cooking. People of the earlier Plains Archaic period used hide or basketry containers, but clay pots represented a great advantage in managing food storage and preparation. Pottery was first developed by eastern and southern Woodland cultures a few hundred years before ceramic technology came to North Dakota.

To make a pot, a skilled potter first identified a good source of clay. The clay was probably located nearby since North Dakota has an abundance of clay soils and clay is too heavy to haul over long distances. The potter had to execute several stages of processing the clay. Raw clay was dried, then pulverized (crushed to fine powder) by pounding it with a hammerstone. Then, the potter removed bits of impurities, sifted the clay powder, added temper material, and finally mixed it with the proper amount of water. Some potters might have let the wet clay age for a few days if the ambient humidity was high enough to prevent the clay from drying.

Tempering was added to the raw clay to strengthen the finished pot. Temper might be sand, crushed rock (grit), crushed shells, or crushed pieces of broken pottery. Adding temper improves the workability of the clay, reduces shrinkage, and decreases the time required for drying the pot. A properly tempered pot is less likely to crack during the firing process. Archaeologists examine the size, quantity, and type of temper to gain more information on the skill of the potter as well as when and where the ceramic piece was made.

Naze potters formed clay into ropes and coiled them to form a pot of the desired size and shape.

The potter kneaded the wet, tempered clay into a uniformly moist and pliable substance. The potter then shaped the pot using one or more of several methods. The techniques most commonly used by Woodland potters were coil, pinch, mold, or paddle anvil.

Coiling was the method chosen by the Naze site potter. To fashion the coiled pot, the potter rolled long ropes from moist clay. These ropes were then coiled, or stacked, one layer upon another. When the pot had assumed the desired size and shape, the potter used the paddle anvil technique to finish shaping and smoothing the pot. To do this, the potter beat the outside of the pot with a paddle while holding a small anvil stone inside the vessel. With this process, the potter consolidated the coils into a thin wall while forcing air bubbles out of the clay and giving the vessel its final shape. The potter fired the pot in hot coals until it was hardened and water-proof. Though clay pots were superior to other containers for cooking and water storage, people continued to make containers of basketry or hide for a variety of uses.

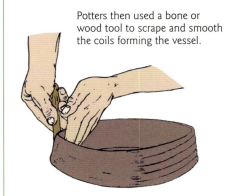

Potters then used a bone or wood tool to scrape and smooth the coils forming the vessel.

The Early Plains Woodland pots varied in size but were generally tall and conical (conoidal) in shape; narrower at the base, wide in the middle, and narrowed slightly toward the top. The conoidal pots did not stand on a flat bottom; they either rested on coals in the fire hearth, or stood on a ring made from hide or plant fibers. These clay pots had relatively thick walls and simple decorations or designs on the outside. The potsherds found in the Naze house had been formed and shaped with a cord-wrapped paddle. Some of the decorated potsherds had trailed lines or punctations made when the potter pressed the wet clay with a stick or other pointed object. The decorations were also pressed into the top and interior of the rim. These designs are similar to those found on pottery made in other Woodland culture communities in southwest Minnesota, Wisconsin, Iowa, and Illinois.

They used a cord-wrapped paddle and anvil to thin the walls and remove air bubbles

The designs on the Naze house pottery were decorative, but also may have been personal identifying marks of the potter. It is also possible that certain types of designs were common to a group of people who shared cultural traits. The ceramic pots found in the Naze house were similar in many ways to pots of the Black Sand tradition found hundreds of miles east and south of North Dakota in Illinois.

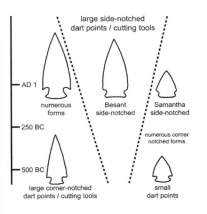

Plains Woodland projectile points were notched on the corners or the sides. Notches made for secure hafting of the point to the shaft.

Fire-cracked rock was altered by heating and often is red or gray and has a friable structure. Stone boiling, steaming, or pit roasting activites are indicated.

Chokecherries, found throughout North Dakota, ripen in August. They were an important source of nutrition for Woodland era peoples.

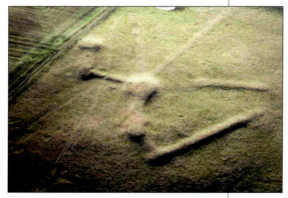

Mortuary rituals of the Plains Woodland era included burying the dead in mounds. This mound complex, known as the Anderson Earthworks, was constructed with both conical mounds and linear mounds.

Archaeologists found a number of corner- or side-notched projectile points among the objects within the burned Naze house. While these points have been difficult to classify, some are similar to Besant side-notched points more commonly found in later Middle Plains Woodland sites. Others may be small Pelican Lake corner-notched points more common to the previous Plains Archaic cultures. Because the points are small, they were attached to lightweight darts and used with an atlatl. A light-weight point launched with a properly weighted atlatl was a deadly weapon when thrust with great force.

The people who lived in the Naze house probably used heated rocks to boil water. Though no well-defined fire pit or hearth was identified in the house, fire-cracked rocks found in the house site indicate cooking techniques that involved heating rocks as had been done for hundreds of years. The people living at the Naze site also butchered animals including bison and elk. Bones of beaver and some species of canine (either domesticated or wild) were also found in the house. The people cooked the broken bones of the large animals to extract the fatty marrow. Materials found in the Naze house include bones, antlers, and wood worked into tools. Naze occupants processed hides to soften them so they could be made into clothing and other objects. They collected plants, including berries and seeds of chokecherry (*Prunus virginiana*), wild grape (*Vitis spp.*), plum (*Prunus Americana*), rose (*Rosa arkansana*), Solomon's seal (*Polygonatum spp.*), lamb's quarters or goosefoot (*Chenopodium*), and marsh elder (*Iva annua*). Some of these plants were, no doubt, used in food preparation, but they may have had medicinal purposes as well. Chokecherry and grape might also have provided dyes or color for decorating objects. Marsh elder might represent early attempts at cultivating wild plants – an initial step in plant domestication.

Archaeologists have identified the Naze house as a "short-term residence" occupied during the fall and winter. The limited number of household objects, a rather small concentration of stone tools and flakes, and the lack of storage pits or stains on the floor suggest the house had not been occupied over a long period of time. It is possible that the housekeeper had removed some debris and cleaned up the hearth just before the fire destroyed the house. But it is also possible this house represented a newly arrived community that was preparing for a winter's stay in the James River bottomlands. What we do not know about that village on the James River is intriguing, but what we have learned from this site is a valuable contribution to the body of knowledge concerning North Dakota's early residents.

Around 100 BC, a significant new cultural tradition appeared marking the transition from Early Plains Woodland to Middle Plains Woodland. The evidence of this transition is seen in the man-made earthen mounds that served as cemetery markers for burials. Mounds are associated with mortuary practices and ceremonies; they suggest that the people of the Middle Woodland period committed their dead to an afterlife with spiritual intentions.

Many mounds have been discovered in the eastern part of North Dakota, particularly along the upland rim of the James and Sheyenne river valleys. Mounds have also been located in similar settings along the Missouri River. They were frequently constructed on high ground overlooking settlements. Some of the mounds were conical, rising in a crown of mounded soil. Often, linear mounds connected conical mounds as part of a burial complex. It is likely that mounds were used for burial of the dead over a very long period of time, perhaps several hundred years. Today, the mounds remain sacred to American Indians and are protected by federal and state laws. Archaeologists avoid excavating mounds whenever possible. If archaeologists find it necessary to open a burial mound, they first consult with tribal authorities and work closely with them during the process.

This conical burial mound is located in eastern North Dakota.

A rare mound excavation took place in 1980 under the supervision of the State Historical Society of North Dakota archaeologists. The mound was endangered by farming, and archaeologists decided it was necessary to excavate the site in order to preserve as much information as possible. The human remains were later reinterred. The mound, located near present-day Inkster in Grand Forks County, contained the skeletal remains of at least twenty-eight individuals, both males and females, ranging from one to fifty-six years of age. The burial of most of these individuals took place after the body had been placed on a scaffold for some time. Later, people, perhaps family members, returned to remove the bones from the scaffold and place them in the mound. This process is called a secondary or bundle burial. A few of the remains found in the Inkster Mound showed evidence of primary burial—that is, these people were buried soon after death and the bodies were not placed on a scaffold. Nearly all remains of people buried at Inkster, both young and old, were prepared for burial with red ochre, a pigment composed mostly of iron oxide. Red ochre is often associated with burial rituals.

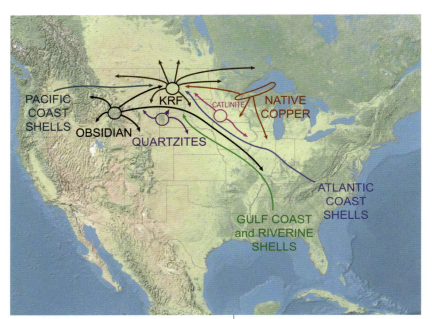

MAP 3.2. Well-established Woodland era trade routes brought goods from across the continent to North Dakota where they were exchanged for Knife River flint.

Catlinite used in this pipe was quarried in southwestern Minnesota.

Ocean shells came to North Dakota through trade. This columella shell was used as a personal ornament.

Copper from the Great Lakes region was made into various tools or ornaments such as this copper disk.

A few of the Inkster burials contained objects that might have held significance for the dead. At another location along the James River, one mound contained ceramics, projectile points, bison remains, copper pieces, columella and other ocean shells, and locally-obtained shells worked into pendants, disks, and gorgets (decorative object worn at the neck).

Archaeologists debate whether mound burial was a ritual reserved for people of high social status or a routine ritual practiced in caring for the dead. Some researchers have noted that fewer remains of women and very young children have been found among the remains placed in the burial mounds; they argue that women and children were purposely excluded from mound burial. Other archaeologists, however, have found no discrepancy in mound burials according to age or sex and none of the burials indicated special status. While present knowledge of burial rituals is limited, it is possible that both sides can claim some measure of truth, depending on the traditions of the society that built and used a particular mound.

Burial mounds and their contents tell us that cultures were often associated with geographic regions. For instance, the mounds found near Arvilla, North Dakota seem to represent a Woodland culture commonly associated with people who, for the most part, lived in the forests of Minnesota. The Arvilla mounds are located at the western edge of their territory. To the north and west, mounds built by the people of the Devils Lake—Sourisford cultural tradition apparently were located at the eastern edge of their range. The goods placed in Devils Lake—Sourisford burials reveal that the people of this tradition had greater opportunities for trade with people from even farther west who brought shells found in the Pacific Ocean. Central North Dakota appears to have been a dividing line between eastern-influenced and western-influenced groups.

Mound building suggests that Woodland cultures were becoming more sedentary and less likely to travel frequently or extensively. The mounds, demanding massive labor and making an emotional and spiritual claim on the people, drew these cultural groups back to the burial sites time and again.

Mounds along the James, Sheyenne, and Missouri rivers were built by people of the Sonota culture who were closely identified with the Middle Plains Woodland complex which lasted from about 100 BC to

AD 600. The people of these cultures were bison hunters and plant gatherers who traveled to familiar places in a seasonal cycle to acquire foods and other resources they needed. They made ceramic pottery very similar to pottery styles found among Midwestern Woodland cultures east of North Dakota.

Sonota cultural artifacts are very similar to those of the Besant cultures that commonly occupied parts of Montana. The two cultures utilized much of the same geographic area in western North Dakota and eastern Montana. Where their ranges overlapped, the cultures are nearly indistinguishable. Artifacts located in Sonota sites include Besant side-notched projectile points and conoidal-shaped ceramic pots. Besant side-notched points, knapped from Knife River flint or other locally sourced stone, tend to be a little larger than Sonota points. Large points, attached to a dart and launched with the aid of an atlatl, had great impact on a bison or elk trapped in a pound or corral. Smaller points would have offered greater dart speed, but reduced impact on the target prey. While there is much similarity in Besant and Sonota artifacts, peoples of Besant cultures did not practice mortuary ceremonialism.

Concurrent occupation of western North Dakota by both Besant and Sonota cultures suggests strong trade networks existed in the western part of the state. Plains Woodland traders exchanged Knife River flint for shells, obsidian, catlinite (red pipestone found in southwestern Minnesota), and possibly food supplies. Flint was highly valued for making tools and was traded to people of Woodland cultures who took the stone to Manitoba and Iowa, and even more distant locations. The people probably also traded for some items that were consumed, worn out through use, or degraded over time and cannot be recovered from archaeological sites. These items may have included bison hides and dried meat. Though trade covered great distances, it does not indicate that people of North Dakota cultures were necessarily in direct contact with Pacific Coast cultures. Trade often involved multiple transactions through many cultures, a process known as "down-the-line" exchange.

Obsidian, a black, glassy stone produced by volcanic activity, has been found in North Dakota's Middle Plains Woodland archaeological sites, most of which was brought from Obsidian Cliff in Yellowstone. A lesser quantity of obsidian was obtained from volcanic flow sources in Idaho. It is not likely that people traveled from the Northern Great Plains to Yellowstone to gather obsidian cobbles; more likely they obtained it through down-the-line or intermediary trade. Obsidian was valued because it could be worked into very sharp-edged points.

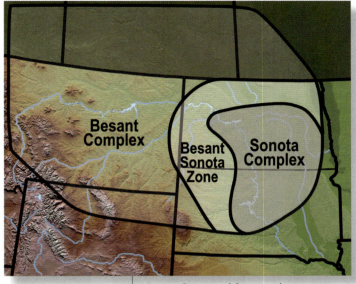

Map 3.3. Besant and Sonota cultures (complexes) overlapped in western North Dakota where each culture was influenced by the traditions of the other.

Middle Plains Woodland ceramic sherds have been recovered from archaeological sites.

This Besant side-notched point with a broken tip shows where the knapper removed flakes to form sharp edges.

Besant points

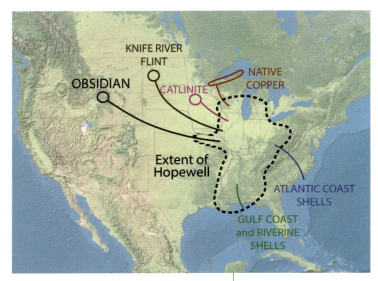

Map 3.4. Hopewell culture and technologies traveled with trade goods to the Northern Great Plains.

Women stitched bison hides together and stretched them over poles to form a tipi. The size of the tipi depended on the size of the family. Dogs harnessed to a travois transported tipis and other goods. *Karl Bodmer painting. Courtesy of the North Dakota Parks and Recreation Department.*

Other objects obtained through trade from the west and south include shells from Pacific Ocean or Gulf Coast sources. However, trade in objects obtained from distant locations did not impact every community in North Dakota. Burials associated with Arvilla populations whose traditions are more closely linked with Minnesota Woodland cultures were likely to include items made from local river mollusk shells than marine shells. The Arvilla population may not have been as likely engage in trade networks as some other groups.

Trade patterns of the Middle Plains Woodland period are not yet well understood, but appear to be rather complex. The presence of exotic trade items and a few projectile points or pots of an exotic style, perhaps made by people of a different or previous culture can be interpreted in several ways. It could be that pieces were left behind by someone and later picked up by people who did not waste any useful thing. It is possible some objects were acquired as the result of raiding. However, peaceful and purposeful exchange is likely responsible for most of the nonlocal objects identified in Middle Plains Woodland archaeological sites. Some archaeologists have proposed that "trade fairs" might have brought people together for peaceful economic and social interaction. Of course, not only were materials and finished goods exchanged, but ideas and skills also moved across social and territorial boundaries resulting in greater cultural complexity of all groups. Conversely, trade probably encouraged people to assume a stronger sense of identity with their cultural or social group which likely resulted in greater social cohesion.

The Hopewell Interaction Sphere may have been a contributing element in the exchange of goods and ideas among North Dakota cultures. Established in forested regions of Ohio and other eastern states, Hopewell cultures (200 BC to AD 500) are known today for impressive mounds, pottery, and exquisite decorative arts. Through a system of exchange not yet fully understood, Hopewell ideas spread far beyond the valleys of central North American rivers such as the Illinois and Scioto. Some of the people who lived in eastern North Dakota were probably influenced by the Hopewell Interaction Sphere, though we don't know if the contact was direct, or if the ideas traveled through other cultures that had direct contact with Hopewell cultures. Certainly, the production of pottery and the practice of mortuary rituals including the building of mounds demonstrate influence from Hopewell cultures.

Though evidence points to increasing attachment to particular locations, Woodland peoples remained primarily nomadic. The economy and success of small communities depended on hunting bison and gathering wild plants. In summer they had to locate near a reliable water source, and in winter they needed shelter from cold wind and storms. At all times, they had to keep watch for approaching travelers, both friendly and hostile. They needed housing that suited all of their needs. The ideal type of house for the nomads of the Woodland era was the tipi.

Women weighted their tipis with stones placed around the lower edge of the hide cover. This stone circle was located in Mercer County and photographed before excavation.

Tipis were typically constructed of poles covered with bison hides. The best tipi poles were cut from lodgepole pine saplings, but few lodgepole pines are found in North Dakota. Ponderosa pines were available, but did not have the ideal diameter for tipis. It is likely that tipi-dwellers chose young aspen or ash trees for their poles. These trees grew almost any place where there was enough moisture in the soil especially along the banks of rivers and creeks. Woodland peoples usually sought high, open ground for their camps. In these sites, the tipis were exposed to the wind and had to be secured to the ground with rocks. While logs, tipi poles, and hide coverings are subject to decay and do not leave traces, the stones that ringed the base of the tipi, provide archaeological evidence of nomadic camps.

Archaeologists excavated the Mercer County stone circle to gather more data on the circle and the people who once lived there.

Stone circles dot the surface of North Dakota's prairie landscape. These are sometimes called tipi rings, but not all stone circles represent the location of a tipi. Some stone circles were constructed for other purposes. However, by examining the archaeological evidence associated with a group of stone circles, archaeologists can determine which sites were camps of tipi-dwelling nomads. One important stone circle site is located in McLean County, on high ground above a coulee (dry gulch) about fifteen miles east of the Missouri River. Today, the site is known as Dancing Grouse.

There are about fifty stone circles at Dancing Grouse. The site was occupied by different groups of people who camped several times in different seasons over a period of several hundred years. The main occupations took place between AD 773 and 944. The people were of the Middle or Late Woodland culture.

Women preparing bison hides for tipi covers scraped flesh from numerous hides and stretched them before stitching them into a tipi cover. *Illustration detail by Rob Evans*

Some stone circles at Dancing Grouse have been disturbed by farming or damming of the river, and some tipi builders "robbed" rocks from earlier structures to set up their tipis. While rocks are abundant in the glacial till (soil and rocks left by receding glaciers) where Dancing Grouse is located, finding and carrying the rocks of the proper size and weight took time and energy. If rocks were already present, the most efficient thing to do was to use rocks from earlier tipi encampments. In spite of the many possibilities for loss or impact to the integrity of stone circles, including weathering, and modern farming or mining, many remain nearly undisturbed. The

Dancing Grouse Tipis by the Numbers

42
The number of complete stone circles

75
Square feet of floor space of the smallest tipi
Who might have lived in the smallest tipi?

669
Square feet of floor space of the largest tipi
What might have been the use of the largest tipi?

11
Number of poles required for the three smallest tipis
About how many dogs would these families need?

28
Number of poles required for the six largest tipis
About how many dogs would these families need?

14
Length (feet) of poles for the three smallest tipis
How does the weight of 14-foot poles compare to the weight of 30-foot poles?

30
Length (feet) of poles for the six largest tipis
How does the weight of 30-foot poles compare to the weight of 14-foot poles?

28
Number of tipis with less than 334.5 square feet of floor space
How does this space compare to a room in your house?

14
Number of tipis with more than 334.5 square feet of floor space
What resources were required to make, maintain, and transport a tipi of this size?

---

site has been preserved well enough to provide a great deal of information about life in the Woodland era.

The residents of Dancing Grouse were bison hunters. The main camp was where most people lived and worked. However, hunters sometimes ranged out from the main village (or base camp) on the coulee to set up small temporary hunting camps about six to twelve miles (ten to twenty kilometers) from the base camp. Hunting camps were temporary and probably involved a small percentage of the main camp's residents. Hunters sought bison and other game and butchered their kills at outlying hunting camps. They brought only meat and necessary bones and organs back to Dancing Grouse. Fire-cracked rock indicates that bones were boiled to extract grease at the main camp, but there is little other evidence to indicate that bison were butchered in the camp.

The main camp was less than fifteen miles from the Missouri River and closer to other small lakes and coulees where fruits and edible plants could be found and gathered. Plant gathering and preserving was likely the work of women as were child rearing and the building and maintenance of the tipis. Archaeologists have found few pieces of bone or stone tools inside the stone circles (representing the inside of the tipis) indicating that Dancing Grouse housekeepers kept their homes clean of debris and refuse. Refuse was deposited outside of the tipi, and most was carried to a high spot where trash was piled.

Women who constructed the tipis utilized their knowledge of prevailing winds and seasonal climates to build tipis that could withstand Northern Plains weather. Tipis appear to be circular, but are actually slightly egg-shaped so that the diameter (or axis) in one direction is a little longer than the diameter in the cross direction. The tipi was placed so that the long axis faced into the prevailing winds (northwest in winter) with the door opening on the opposite side from the winds. Rocks were piled more heavily on the side facing the prevailing winds in order to prevent damage from high winds. Spring and summer winds are more likely to come from the southwest so the women aligned the axis and distributed the rocks accordingly. In summer, however, fewer stones were used on the tipi walls so that the lower edges could be raised for air circulation inside the tipi. By examining the shape and alignment of the stone circles, archaeologists have found that Dancing Grouse was occupied at different times of the year. Eventually, tipi-dwellers used wood stakes or bone pins to secure a tipi to the ground, but even with the metal stakes available hundreds of years later, dry-hard or frozen ground still called for rocks to secure the tipi against the wind.

The size of the tipi varied with the size of the family and the purpose of the structure. The largest tipis were sometimes used as council lodges or ceremonial lodges, or perhaps as dwellings for a group of unmarried men. The largest tipi at Dancing Grouse was more than twenty-nine feet (8.9 meters) in diameter, while the smallest was just under ten feet (3.4 meters) in diameter. The covers were tanned bison hides stitched together. Mid-sized tipis required six to fourteen hides to make the cover, but the largest tipis might have needed twenty hides. These large tipi covers were probably constructed as two pieces that were joined on the tipi, so that they could be transported in two lighter-weight segments.

Coyote, dog, and wolf skeletal (l to r) remains are shown for the sake of comparison. *Photo courtesy of Abigail Fisher, specimens are from the SMU Anthropology Zooarchaeological Comparative Collection.*

Tipis are mobile housing units, but the larger the tipi, the greater the weight. A family had to be able to efficiently transport tipi poles, cover, and all the family's material goods (but not the stone weights) from one site to another. Dogs carried the tipis and other goods either in packs on their backs or as part of a travois system. A travois consisted of a pair of long poles with a woven, flat basket lashed between the poles to carry the load. The travois was harnessed to a mature dog that could carry or pull forty to fifty pounds. Some archaeologists estimate that an average family of two to three adults and three to four children might have kept as many as eight working dogs plus a few puppies, pets, or breeding females. That might amount to as many as one hundred dogs for one of the communities that lived at Dancing Grouse. All of these dogs had to be fed, drawing on resources that were sometimes hard to acquire.

Travel was an integral part of the nomadic economy. The entire group sometimes had to travel when they needed to locate bison herds, plants in season, or stone quarries. The distance a group could travel in a day with all of their goods was limited by the weight they had to transport and by the number and health of the dogs carrying the load. Archaeologists, calculating the weight of goods and the strength of dogs, estimate that a day's travel might have been less than five miles. The limitations of foot travel aided by dogs suggest that a Plains Woodland family could not afford to build a tipi larger than the family required, keep more dogs than they needed for transport, or move more often than necessary. Every decision had a cost and those costs were carefully calculated.

People of the Northern Great Plains adopted bow and arrow technology around AD 600. Arrows traveled with great speed and power, but many hunters used an atlatl and dart for many more years.

Prairie Side-notched points varied in size and shape (above and below).

Avonlea points were small. Some archaeologists have said that they were the most beautifully crafted of Woodland era projectile points.

Triangular unnotched points were generally small and were inserted in a groove at the end of an arrow.

The people who lived at Dancing Grouse preferred Knife River flint for their dart points, but they also used Tongue River Silicified Sediment (TRSS) for points and other tools. There is little evidence for stone working inside the tipis. They either made points and tools outside of the tipis or the housekeepers carried the debris away from the house to a refuse dump. It is likely that women carefully cleaned the tipis because there are few pieces of broken ceramics (just enough to know that they made and used pottery) or broken bone. The absence of artifacts within the tipi circles can possibly be attributed to more recent artifact-hunters, but the consistent absence of material goods within the excavated circles supports the cleanliness theory.

Throughout this time period, the people of Dancing Grouse and all other cultural groups who lived on the Northern Great Plains continued to pursue an economy based on bison hunting and plant gathering, each in its own season. It was a pattern well-established by their ancestors. However, they also experimented with new skills, innovations, and ideas, adopting those that seemed an improvement over old ways and modifying some to suit them. By AD 600, traditions had changed sufficiently for archaeologists to identify and differentiate a new complex of cultures they call Late Plains Woodland (AD 600 to 1200). During this time period, people constructed mounds less often, but they sometimes used existing mounds for burials. They also advanced in pottery technology and adopted new decorative modes of design. In addition, changes in weaponry and social organization emerged laying the foundation for new adaptations and lifeways on the Northern Great Plains.

Around AD 600, hunters on the Northern Great Plains began to use the bow and arrow, a weapon system requiring new skills in manufacture and use. Peoples occupying regions north and west of North Dakota had used the bow and arrow hundreds of years earlier, but the new technology made its way slowly into the Northern Great Plains, bringing some advantages in weaponry, but not completely replacing the dart and atlatl.

Archaeologists have determined that bow and arrow technology was introduced around AD 600 because projectile points became much smaller and thinner in this time period. Arrow points were so much smaller than dart points that several of these projectile tips might be knapped from a single, relatively small piece of stone. Points found in archaeological sites dating to the Late Plains Woodland era were crafted in a variety of styles including side-notched and triangular (unnotched). Each type of point had its advantages. Notched points, lashed securely to the arrow, were likely to penetrate the target without breaking, but demanded more time and skill for manufacturing. Triangular, unnotched points were inserted into a groove or slit at the end of the arrow. The unnotched shape could be manufactured quickly, but it could break away from the shaft on contact with the target. It appears that knappers still preferred Knife River flint for arrow points, but other types of stone, either locally acquired or procured through trade networks, also appear in archaeological sites.

Archaeologists agree that the size and weight of projectile points indicate that small points were made for bow and arrow. Research shows that an arrow point typically weighed about .17 ounces (5 grams). Anything heavier traveled more slowly and with less power, and was therefore a less effective weapon. The power of a tautly strung bow launched a lightweight arrow toward the target with greater speed and longer range than was possible with a dart and atlatl. In hunting quick and wary prey such as deer or antelope, the hunter's ability to quickly and accurately launch an arrow was a great asset.

Arrows also had the advantage of traveling in a somewhat flatter trajectory toward the target than a hand-thrown dart. It was easier to send an arrow to the proper place (the "kill zone") on the prey animal than with a dart, an important factor for younger or less skilled hunters. The kill zone (the heart and lungs) on a large deer is about twelve inches (thirty centimeters) in diameter. On a bison, the same area is more than twice as large, about twenty-eight inches (seventy-one centimeters). These figures might suggest that a bison made an easier target, but the projectile had to pass through dense, heavy hide and penetrate farther into the body cavity in order to be effective. Light-weight arrows launched from a well-strung bow were as likely to mortally wound or kill bison as the heavier darts of the atlatl system.

Some hunters using bow and arrow technology developed a new style of point, very small, and arguably among the most carefully crafted points since the Folsom point. This point was associated with the Avonlea culture (AD 500 to 800) which thrived in the central portion of North Dakota. The Avonlea projectile point was side-notched, very symmetrical, and had a slightly concave base. Avonlea knappers carefully controlled the flaking process to make this tiny, well-formed point. It is possible that the knapping skill required to fashion an Avonlea point was linked to rituals associated with hunting.

Just as Woodland era hunters knew the behavior and habitats of the game they pursued, they knew the different qualities of each type of wood they chose for arrow shafts. They favored fruitwood such as juneberry (*Amelanchier alnifolia*) or chokecherry. Fruitwood branches had to be smoothed and straightened into arrow shafts that would travel accurately. A skilled hunter's toolkit included a stone spokeshave tool and a shaft-wrench made from a drilled or perforated bison rib bone to make a branch into an arrow shaft by removing all naturally-occurring knobs and curves. After drilling a hole of the proper diameter through the bone, the hunter drew the shafts through the hole and pulled them back and forth to form a smooth, straight arrow.

Juneberry arrows are dense and relatively heavy, but Woodland hunters found that they did not break easily and carried through heavy winds

Holes were drilled through these bones so that they could be used to straighten and smooth arrow shafts. A stick would be drawn several times through the hole of the arrow shaft straightener to wear away irregularities.

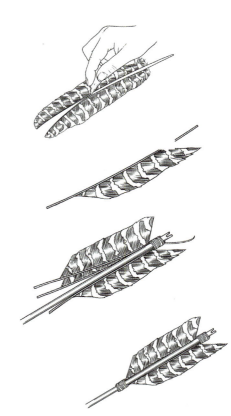

Feathers were attached to balance the weight of the point. Hunters preferred feathers of eagles, hawks, or geese. Fletching was attached with a wrap of sinew or with glue.

Companion Dogs

At some time in the past, some wolves became domesticated. No one knows how it happened, but the result was the dog—a gentler, dopier version of the wolf. Domestication of the wolf might have happened somewhere in Asia around twenty thousand years ago, before or perhaps around the same time that people began to immigrate to North America over the Bering Land Bridge. The dates and locations are fuzzy and scientists using DNA tests are not yet able to clarify any specifics as to time and place.

Geneticists studying the evolution of dogs and modern wolves have determined that they share a common wolf ancestor. However, that ancestor was genetically different from modern wolves (*Canis lupus*) and modern dogs (*Canis lupus familiaris*). Scientists currently consider two possibilities to explain the evolution of dogs. The first is that dogs biologically evolved from wolves and were adopted by humans because they found the characteristics of dogs desirable. Alternatively, some wolves allowed themselves to become domesticated and in time, through a variety of natural processes, underwent genetic changes that are now characteristic of poodles and bull mastiffs.

A major distinction between dogs and wolves is that dogs can digest starches (found in plants) and wolves cannot. Scientists theorize that plant- and meat-eating dogs could find more to eat among the scraps of human food than wolves which eat only meat. Dogs also fail to develop a full range of adult canine qualities; an adult dog has the mental age of a ten-week-old wolf pup making dogs gentler and less aggressive than an adult wolf.

Scientists are still working their way through the maze of genetic and archaeological puzzles concerning the domestication of dogs, but thousands of years ago, dog owners recognized that dogs could shoulder some of the work load, guard the village, and provide companionship.

with greater accuracy than lighter weight arrows. Chokecherry branches were less dense, and lighter in weight than juneberry wood. To prepare arrows, the hunter had to select a point that matched the weight of the wood he chose. The hunter had to know what game he would be hunting and what circumstances would prevail during the hunt in order to choose the best wood for the arrow.

Arrows also had to be fletched, a process some hunters had used on atlatl darts. Fletching is the application of bird feathers to end of the arrow opposite the projectile tip to balance the weight of the point. Feathers of relatively large birds including eagle, crow, goose, or hawk were often selected for fletching. The hunter could attach a portion of the feather shaft to the arrow and secure it by wrapping it with sinew—connective tissue taken from animals during the butchering process and saved for this purpose. Another method was to strip the barbs (soft colorful parts of the feather) from the shaft and glue them to the arrow before wrapping them with sinew. The latter method created a faster arrow, but it was a more time-consuming process.

Woodland era hunters also had to understand how to make a bow that worked properly. Bows had to be flexible and bend, but not break, when drawn. Hunters favored locally available woods such as chokecherry, oak (*Quercus macrocarpa*), juniper (*Juniperus scopulorum*), and juneberry. Some bows might have been reinforced with sinew, or constructed with sinew and elk antler or bison horn. The pieces added to the wood were attached with glue made from hide. These composite forms are referred to as backed bows.

The bow string was made from a variety of materials. One type of bow string was made from sinew, especially a long section taken from the back bone or back leg of a large deer, elk, or bison. Hunters also used rawhide or gut material to manufacture bowstrings. Some hunters twisted plant fibers into cord that made a strong and effective bowstring, but the process was slow. The plants had to be harvested, shredded into strips of the proper length, and twisted into a cord of the appropriate diameter. Ease and speed of manufacture were often determining factors in selecting materials.

Woodland hunters probably viewed the bow and arrow with some skepticism at first. After all, they could not chance an unsuccessful hunt since bison were a major source of food, clothing, tools, and other useful objects. For hundreds of years, people of all Great Plains cultures had organized their communities and their annual cycle of events around communal bison hunting. The bow and arrow gave an advantage to an individual hunter who stalked deer and other mid- to small-sized game. Initially, however, the bow and arrow was a weapon of limited use. The dart and atlatl continued to be widely used for hundreds of years after the introduction of the bow and arrow for both individual hunts and for the seasonal communal hunts.

Traditional communal hunts were carefully organized. Several small groups came together for the summer hunt. Most of the year, communities comprised perhaps seventy to one hundred people, but at the gathering for a communal hunt, the entire group of friends and relatives formed a huge camp of several hundred people. The summer hunt yielded the meat, bone, hide, and internal organs of several hundred bison cows, bulls, and calves—enough to supply the communities until they gathered again for the fall hunt.

There were a few different options for hunting large numbers of bison. Men, women, and children worked together to construct hidden, brush-covered corrals (called "pounds") along a known bison trail. Hazers drove the animals toward the pound. Once enclosed, the confused animals circled as the hunters launched their darts and spears toward the kill zone (heart and lungs) on each animal. A similar method made use of a small canyon or draw to corral and trap a herd. Everyone helped in the processing of the carcasses.

Hunters also trapped bison at muddy watering holes. Though good swimmers, muddy shores slowed the heavy animals long enough for hunters to kill them. During the winter, hunters ran bison into deep snow banks where their short legs were of no use. Hunters could take advantage of another winter-time hunting technique when they found a herd on ice, where their hooves could not gain purchase to propel them out of range of the hunters' darts.

Most dramatically, massive, highly organized, and carefully coordinated hunts brought a herd slowly and deliberately across a plain toward a cliff or the high bank of a small river. The hunters were divided into task groups. Keeping in mind that bison could run at a steady pace for miles, the hunt organizers posted many hunters along the designated trail. A few boys and men started the herd moving the right direction and individuals posted along the trail hazed the herd to keep it running between cairns (stone markers) that marked the path toward the cliff. Near the cliff's edge, hazers frightened the herd into a stampede which propelled the animals over the cliff to their deaths below. At the base of the cliff, hunters found animals that had not died from the fall, and finished them off. Women waited with knives to butcher the carcasses.

All methods of hunting were dangerous. Hunters had to approach close enough to the animals or the herd so their weapons could pierce the thick, woolly coat and hide. An aggressive, wounded bison bull or cow could spin quickly toward perceived danger and charge rapidly into the hunters. Bison, wild with fear, could jump corral fences and trample hunters. Hunters had to know how a bison might react in order to avoid being gored or trampled by frightened animals. A successful hunt depended on the hunters taking advantage of bison herd behavior and, at the same time, blunting the animals' best defenses of speed and aggression.

Broken pieces of Late Plains Woodland pottery were fitted together to show how the pot was shaped and decorated.

The territory of the Blackduck tradition extended into northeastern North Dakota. They made rounded, thin-walled pots. This Blackduck pot was decorated with a cord-wrapped tool.

All of the cultural groups living on the Northern Great Plains in the Late Plains Woodland period organized bison hunts in similar fashion. During this time period, however, co-existing cultural groups in the region developed distinctive lifeways that were particularly apparent in their lithic and ceramic technology. For instance, the Avonlea culture, associated with the Avonlea point, was also known for its distinctive ceramic style.

Avonlea pots, like others of the Late Woodland period, were made with thinner walls than earlier styles. These tall pots were large enough to hold several gallons of water or other liquids. While some pots had the older conical shape, others were rounded, but flattened on the bottom so they stood upright. Potters generally produced Avonlea pots by pressing slabs of prepared, tempered clay into the desired shape. Fingerprints remain on the inside of some pots showing how the potter worked the clay into the proper shape.

Avonlea pots are distinguished by three common decorative modes or styles. The potter sometimes pressed netting or basketry over the exterior of the pot before firing. Potters of another style, called parallel grooved, imprinted pots with grooves running horizontally around the pot surface. The potter might have used a carved paddle to make neat, evenly spaced grooves in the clay. The third common decoration found on Avonlea pots is called cord-wrapped tool-impressed. This design was achieved by applying a cord-wrapped stick vertically down the pot. In addition, potters decorated their vessels with punctated (a mark poked into the clay), embossed, or other impressions in the clay, usually near the rim at the top of the pot.

This aerial photo of Menoken village shows the ditch and bastions that protected the village. Apple Creek on the north and west sides formed a natural boundary. A depression marks the excavation of a house.

Another culture, known today as Blackduck, was located primarily in northeastern North Dakota. People of the Blackduck tradition are known for their distinctive ceramic vessels. These thin-walled pots were usually globular (rounded) in shape. The potters decorated their vessels with elaborate designs applied with cord-wrapped tools on the lip and the rim. They added punctate designs to make elegant, but practical vessels.

While the production of useful and beautiful pots eased housekeeping chores in many ways and possibly enhanced the potter's status in her (or his) community, evidence indicates many women continued to use age-old ways of preparing food. Archaeologists have found firepits where rocks were heated before being placed in skin containers to boil water; at the same sites archaeologists have also found fired-clay pots. As with weaponry, people did not quickly abandon traditional technologies for new-fangled methods or innovations. After all, pots could break and spoil a good meal.

The population of North Dakota grew throughout the Late Plains Woodland period. Peoples of distinct cultures lived as neighbors in the region leaving a jigsaw puzzle of cultural evidence for archaeologists to sort out. Cultural evidence is sometimes found far from where it might be expected. When archaeologists found a few pieces of cord-wrapped, stick-impressed pottery in Billings County (not far from Grassy Butte), far to the west of where pottery was usually manufactured and used, they had to consider possible explanations for the location of these potsherds. While there is much evidence for human occupation of the badlands in the Late Plains Woodland era, there is little evidence that people who lived in or regularly visited the badlands worked with ceramics. How did those pieces of pottery arrive in the badlands? Was there a trade system that brought potters together with nomadic peoples who had little time for pot making? Or did people travel to the badlands to hunt and leave a broken pot behind when they returned home? It is impossible to know exactly how it happened, but the broken pottery in the badlands tells us that cultural encounters and exchange took place across the expanse of North Dakota and that every group felt the influence of other cultures of the region.

A painting of Menoken village is based on archaeological investigations. *Illustration by Becky Barnes*

As the Late Plains Woodland period drew to a close in western North Dakota, a group of people established a small village on the banks of Apple Creek about ten miles east of Bismarck. This village is now known as Menoken Indian Village, a State Historic Site. About two hundred men, women, and children lived in this village occupying thirty oval-shaped, earth-covered lodges built in at least two different architectural styles. The steep banks of Apple Creek protected the north and west sides of the village. On the south and east sides, a palisade (wall) and ditch fortification system enclosed the one and one-half acre village. The palisade included several bastions (projections) from which watchers could observe activities beyond the village. We do not know if they built a fortified village because they felt a need to protect themselves from hostile groups or if they wanted to control access to their village when nomadic neighbors stopped by. Maybe they considered both possibilities as they lifted the logs of the fortification into place.

Two of the houses at Menoken Village have been excavated by archaeologists. One of these houses, House 2, was built in a pit dug about two feet into the ground. Three upright posts supported a ridge beam running the length of the house. The roof and walls were covered with earth; the walls may have been built of stacked sod. Timber posts and a lintel framed the southwest-facing doorway. A ramp entrance sloped down to the earthen living floor.

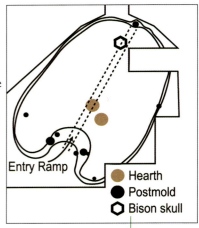

The people who built House 2 at Menoken village dug a pit so that the floor of the house was lower than the surrounding ground surface.
House 2 plan.

The pit construction was evident when House 2 was excavated.

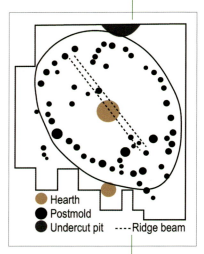

House 17 was constructed in a different manner than House 2. It was built on the surface using poles to support the walls. The plan map shows placement of supporting timbers.
House 17 plan.

House 17 was one of two houses excavated at Menoken.

The housekeeper of House 2 kept items that were not used daily at the back of the house (opposite the door). These included a bison skull, red ochre pigment, and a variety of broken tools. The family also stored items on the roof, suggesting the roof sloped down close enough to the ground for easy access. Several hearths, for outdoor cooking or firing ceramic vessels, were found outside of the house. The residents deposited their trash in pits near the house.

A structurally different house, House 17, was occupied at about the same time as House 2. It was not a pit house, but was built on the natural ground surface. The house was oval in shape and about twenty-three feet by seventeen feet, just a little larger than House 2. On the southeast side of the lodge was an entryway framed by upright posts. The elm and oak roof beams were supported by posts that formed the periphery of the lodge. The posts were set into holes dug in the ground and secured or chinked with bison bones and fire-cracked rock. The roof was covered with branches and eight to twelve inches of earth. The sides of the house were made of earth. The residents of this house, too, stored tools and a small cache of flint cobbles (for manufacturing new tools) at the back of the house. They used the roof to store large stone tools and probably had easy access to the low-sloped roof. Among the outdoor pits and fire hearths was a large, bell-shaped pit (cache pit) which might have been used for storing dried foodstuffs for future use. The central hearth inside the lodge had been used to burn wood from elm, box elder, oak, and willow trees. These trees, along with ash trees, grew nearby on the forested banks of Apple Creek.

The people of Menoken Village made their stone tools from Knife River flint and Tongue River Silicified Sediment (TRSS). Though obtaining Knife River flint required a journey of 130 miles and TRSS was available about thirty miles away, the villagers apparently thought it worth the effort to go to the flint quarries because ninety percent of their stone tools and arrow points were knapped from flint.

The residents of Menoken Village engaged in trade through extensive systems that connected them to people who brought highly valued "exotic" trade goods to the region. While it is unlikely that the people of Menoken Village traveled to the East or Gulf Coast for shells or the Great Lakes region for copper, they met and traded with people through the pattern of "down-the-line" exchange who had previously met people who had something interesting to trade. Among the trade goods found in Menoken Village are shells of marine animals commonly found in the Caribbean Sea, Gulf of Mexico, or Atlantic Ocean. The iridescent shells made beautiful beads and pendants, but could also be sharpened into awls or other useful tools.

Menoken Village is the first known permanent village in North Dakota. Construction of the earth-covered lodges and the palisade required a substantial investment in labor and materials. These structures were built to shelter village residents for several years. Though they had become more sedentary than their ancestors and many other peoples of the northern Great Plains, the people of Menoken Village continued to rely on bison for a major portion of their diet just as their ancestors had. They had to leave the village to hunt at the proper season and return with the hides, bones, and meat. They also gathered plants in season. However, there was something very different in the food supply in this village. Among the charred remains of a hearth, archaeologists found some kernels of corn. While there is no evidence that the people of Menoken Village raised crops in or near their village, they had certainly come into contact with people who either grew corn or engaged in trade with horticultural peoples. Their permanent village and sedentary life opened the door to horticulture and the cultivation of garden crops.

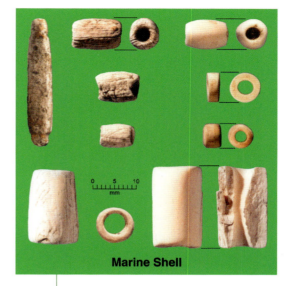

Marine Shell

Multiple and distinct Plains Woodland cultures thrived in North Dakota throughout a period of more than 1,600 years. Over this time period, peoples of the Woodland cultures became more sedentary than the earlier residents of North Dakota. They hunted and gathered plants, traded, and located necessary resources within a relatively small range, visiting and revisiting familiar places regularly. They remained tied to the region by ancestral roots which they maintained by building mounds and using them for burials for hundreds of years.

Marine shell and copper artifacts were among the transcontinental trade items recovered at Menoken.

But these increasingly sedentary peoples were not isolated. The presence of trade goods from across the continent suggests a cosmopolitan world view and an interest in acquiring new ideas, skills, and material goods. Each culture of the Plains Woodland traditions exerted some influence over the others, allowing each group to advance in food production, housing, and weaponry in its own way. Menoken Village was the product of all of the ideas that were adopted or developed among the Plains Woodland cultures, and in that little village people came to know corn, the stepping stone to a major economic change that had broad social and spiritual implications for succeeding generations.

Archaeologists recovered pottery from the Menoken site that displays manufacturing and stylistic characteristics of both the Plains Woodland period and Plains Village period.

People were making and using fired clay vessels during the Plains Woodland period.

Plains Woodland Period Timeline
400 BC to AD 1700s

	NORTH DAKOTA	NORTH AMERICA	WORLD
BC/AD			— First British inoculation against smallpox
AD 1700		— Plymouth Colony	
AD 1500	— Sandy Lake Complex AD 1000-1700	— Horses return to North America — Columbus lands on Caribbean Islands	— Inca Empire, South America
AD 1350		— Aztec Empire, Mesoamerica — Little Ice Age AD 1300-1850	— Great Famine in northern Europe
AD 1200	— Menoken Site — Flaming Arrow Site	— Mississippian Culture AD 800-1600 — Cahokia at its peak AD 1050-1250	
AD 950		— Chaco Canyon Pueblos AD 900-1150 — Vikings settle Greenland	
AD 750	— Black Duck Complex AD 800-1400 — Dancing Grouse Site	— Bow and arrow widely adapted	— Gunpowder invented, China
AD 550	— Arvilla Complex AD 600-900 — Avonlea Complex AD 500-1000		
AD 320			— Period of warfare and migration in Europe known as the Dark Ages
AD 120	— Besant / Sonota Cultural Complex 100 BC-AD 600	— Hopewell cultures 200 BC-AD 500	— Smallpox epidemic ravages the Roman Empire — Rome's Colosseum opens, Italy
AD 1			— Birth of Jesus Christ — First Great Wall built, China
350 BC	— Moderately moist habitat — Naze Site (Early Woodland Component)	— Adena Culture 500 BC-AD 100	— Birth of Buddha

Late Woodland AD 600-1700s
Middle Woodland 100 BC - AD 600
Early Woodland 400-100 BC

The Smithsonian Institution River Basin Surveys

In 1944, Congress appropriated funds to a massive dam-building program called the Pick-Sloan Plan. Under the plan, the federal government proposed to build several dams on the Missouri River to mitigate flooding, improve navigation on the lower Missouri River, provide water for irrigation, and harness power for electrical generation. Recreation was a distant afterthought, but today recreation in the form of fishing and boating on the Lake Sakakawea and Lake Oahe are major attractions for North Dakota residents.

With work on the dams underway, the Smithsonian Institution in partnership with the National Park Service, state historical societies, and research universities responded to concerns of archaeologists and paleontologists about the loss of important historical and scientific information that might be covered by the lakes or destroyed by earthworks. The Smithsonian initiated an equally massive effort, called the River Basin Surveys (RBS), to identify, record, and/or excavate as many as possible of the endangered historical and archaeological sites along the Missouri River.

The surveys resulted in several important advances in archaeological methods. Archaeologists developed a system for identifying sites that remains in place today. Called the "trinomial system," each site received a unique number that identified the state, the county, and the individual site. So, Double Ditch State Historic Site is also known to archaeologists as 32BL8. North Dakota's number is 32; Burleigh County is BL; Double Ditch is site 8. Like Double Ditch, most sites also have a name, but the trinomial designation is specific to one site and never duplicated or misleading.

Another process developed by the archaeologists who worked for the RBS was the development of a more precise system of taxonomy (categorization) that brought order to the overwhelming quantity of information about sites, dates, and locations in the Middle Missouri River region. This volume does not apply all levels of categories for the Plains Village Tradition because of their complexity, but archaeologists depend on this system to organize their analysis of the prehistory of central North Dakota and other Missouri River archaeological sites.

Faced with rising waters behind six dams, archaeologists worked rapidly. They set priorities, concentrating on the physical organization of each village and the architecture of the houses. They excavated one or two houses, if possible, and collected artifacts from excavations and from the surface. Millions of artifacts, including worked stone, bone, shell, wood, and ceramic pieces, were placed in the Smithsonian Institution, the State Historical Society of North Dakota, and other regional collections for preservation. These collections are yielding new information when examined by modern scientific methods and analyzed in light of the accumulating knowledge about the Plains Village era.

The RBS operated from 1946 to 1969 on the Upper Missouri River Basin. In 1969, the program was turned over to the National Park Service where it was renamed the Midwest Archaeological Center. The Center continued the work of the RBS on a smaller scale, but since 1975, it has conducted archaeological investigations only for the National Park Service.

Archaeologists working for the RBS excavated about two hundred sites in North Dakota and South Dakota. The plan was ambitious, the work was hurried, and some sites received more attention than others creating challenges for archaeologists who want to analyze the breadth of Plains Village Culture. Nevertheless, the River Basin Surveys fostered the collection of information and preservation of artifacts from sites that have since disappeared. Though the survey fell short in some ways, archaeologists continue to draw upon the collections now safely housed in the collections of public institutions to further an understanding of the people who came to the Missouri River valley hundreds of years ago seeking a good life.

MAP 3.5. Map of the locations of communities now under Lake Sakakawea.

CONSTRUCTION OF THE GARRISON DAM

The dam on the Missouri River created Lake Sakakawea providing flood control downstream, electrical generation, and recreation.

Lake Sakakawea and Lake Oahe flooded many archaeological sites as well as homes and farms of members of the Mandan, Hidatsa, and Arikara nations.

Aerial view of Like-a-Fishhook village of the Mandan, Hidatsa, and Arikara peoples being inundated by Lake Sakakawea in the early 1950s.

Huff Village was one of numerous sites excavated by the River Basin Surveys. This is a photograph of one of the several houses excavated at the site in 1960 in anticipation of wave action impacts once Oahe Reservoir reached full pool elevation.

Chapter 4

People of the Earthlodges

Plains Village Cultures
AD 1200 to 1785

Where they gathered—Arikara—
they danced and sang.
They are thankful for the
corn that has come.
One stalk of corn is put
on top of the altar.
The one standing the
corn stalk it represents Mother Corn.
She is the one that is sacred.

iinaraakaawiítlt sahniš
nakukaawaáhu na naraahnaanoóku
tiraasšteehuú'U sahniš
wetiraana' neešu
Axku neeštaatu' tlhuucitakUx
huuknaanu
Anuunaaricl neeštaátu'
tuutaweewí'u atina
neešu nikuti nawaawaruxti

— Four Rings, Arikara, 1924

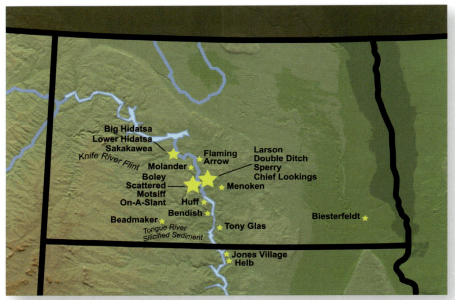

Map 4.1. Most earthlodge villages were located on the Missouri River or one of its tributaries. The large stars represent the location of several village sites; small stars represent individual village sites.

The people at Menoken hunted bison, made pottery, lived in permanent earth-covered houses, and ate (but did not regularly cultivate) corn and other garden crops. However, just a few years earlier, about two hundred miles to the south, at a site now identified as Jones Village, residents lived in much the same way as the people of Menoken, but they also raised corn, beans, and squash to supplement and diversify their food supply. The people at Jones Village lived in earthlodges and had an economy based on hunting, gathering, and raising crops. Their villages and those of their kin were located along the middle section of the Missouri River though their cultural traits likely originated farther south and east. The people who lived at Jones may have pushed northward into what is today North Dakota and met other groups of people who were interested in their subsistence strategies, technologies, and ideas, especially raising corn and other garden produce.

People living at Menoken were part of what archaeologists refer to as the terminal Late Plains Woodland tradition in the Missouri River region. They had not yet adopted or developed methods for the cultivation of corn, but corn kernels found in the village indicate that they were in contact with corn-growing cultures and acquired crops through trade. Menoken villagers and their neighbors also adopted new technologies in ceramics and housing. This adaptive strategy is seen at a site called Flaming Arrow some forty miles northwest of Menoken along the Missouri River. The people of these villages eventually adopted the practice of growing crops which enabled them to store the surplus, build permanent houses (as opposed to tipis), and live in settlements for as long as the location suited them.

Multiple cultural processes were at work among the peoples of central North Dakota by AD 1200. The years leading up to the Plains Village period were a dynamic time. People moved around the region to hunt, trade, quarry flint, and, ultimately settle in a chosen location. They likely met people of other traditions on these journeys and came away with new ideas and skills. During the six hundred years of the Plains Village period substantial changes occurred in population size, settlement plans, architecture, and technologies. Remaining consistent for centuries was the cultivating and harvesting of garden produce. Crop surpluses were instrumental in villages becoming large trading centers where people acquired skills for navigating trading transactions. The Plains Village tradition came to dominate the region of the Missouri River valley and its tributaries. It was a new lifeway that combined the old ways of bison hunting and plant gathering with the new cultural traits and traditions of village settlements and the cultivation of crops, also known as horticulture.

It is not possible to assign to any group of people in the earlier archaeological cultural periods a modern tribal affiliation. The objects that archaeologists use to identify ancient cultures tell us very little about language, worldview or religious perspective, social organization, or group cohesion. All of these characteristics that define a particular culture become clearer during the Plains Village era. It is in this time period, that archaeologists note the emergence of three distinct tribes among the Plains Village groups. The archaeological record of pottery styles and village architecture and organization synchronizes well with Mandan, Hidatsa, and Arikara oral traditions that point to places where important events happened in their respective tribal histories. Oral traditions and archaeological records also match well with the histories recorded by European traders and explorers who reached the villages as early as 1738.

The origin stories of both the Mandans and Hidatsas tell how people migrated to the Missouri River valley from other areas as well as how people originated or came into being in this area. The Mandans have two creation stories. The first tells of emerging from the earth at the mouth of the Mississippi River and migrating north until reaching the Heart River along the Missouri River. The second creation story speaks of people originating at the Heart River (the heart or center of their world). This story explains how the terrain came about as Lone Man created flat grassland interspersed with lakes and areas of timber. He placed many animals to the north and east. Meanwhile, First Creator went south and west, making rugged badlands with streams, hills, and herds of bison. The two then created women and men to populate the land.

In the beginning, Mandan society had four or five social divisions; these collapsed into two main divisions by the late 1700s. Each of the divisions spoke a different dialect of the Mandan language and lived in vil-

Corn

Corn (*Zea mays*) was unknown to Europeans before they arrived in the Americas in 1492. Corn, also known as maize, is a plant with ancient origins in the highlands of central Mexico. A type of grass, corn kernels are seventy-two percent starch, ten percent protein, and five percent oil – an excellent resource of both calories and nutrition.

Maize resulted from the domestication of *teosinte* perhaps ten thousand years ago. Olmec farmers in Mexico cultivated corn as early as six thousand years ago. Through selection of desired seed characteristics and natural processes, corn became a food staple in Mexico by 1300 BC.

Over hundreds of years, corn traveled with people into what is today the American Southwest. In New Mexico, Hopis, Zunis, and other Puebloan peoples cultivated corn and incorporated it symbolically into their ceremonies. Corn moved slowly into the Great Plains and, over hundreds of years, became adapted to cold climates and short growing seasons on the Northern Plains. Along with bison hunting, corn became a staple of a dual system of food production that assured people of a reliable food supply throughout the year.

When naturalist John Bradbury ascended the Missouri River to the Arikara villages in 1811, he found corn fields that amazed him: "I have not seen," he wrote, ". . . any crop of Indian corn in finer order or better managed than the corn about the[se] three villages." Later, Bismarck horticulturist Oscar Will saw the value in corn that had been cultivated and selected for the northern climate by generations of Arikara women farmers. He included a variety of Arikara corn in his first seed catalog, so that pioneer farmers would have access to corn bred for the region's climate. Today, we still place significance on corn for its high nutritional value and the pleasure of biting into an ear of sweet corn on a hot summer day.

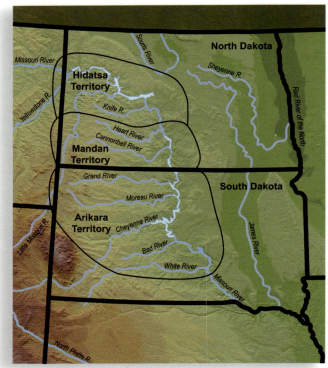

Map 4.2. During the Plains Village era, the Mandans, Hidatsas, and Arikaras lived in distinct territories along the Missouri River.

lages close to one another. At the Heart River area, the Nuitadi (Nueta dialect speakers) occupied the traditional west bank villages (On-A-Slant, Motsiff, Scattered, and Boley), whereas the east bank villages (Chief Lookings, Sperry, Double Ditch, and Larson) were occupied by the Nuptadi (Ruptare dialect speakers).

Originally, there were three subgroups of Hidatsas. One group, the Awatixa (ah wah TEE hah), always lived near the mouth of the Knife River along the Missouri River according to their oral traditions. Their first village may have been the Flaming Arrow settlement. Later, the Awaxawi (ah wah HAH wee) migrated to the Knife River villages from locations somewhere to the east, as did a third group, the Hidatsa-proper, a little later. The oral traditions of the Awaxawi and Hidatsa-proper describe their creation in a world beneath the waters of a large lake, unlike the Awatixas who came from the sky world. The three groups of Hidatsas spoke different dialects of the same stock language and had many cultural traits in common. Both the Mandans and the Hidatsas spoke a language related to the Siouan family of languages. While their languages were distinct, they were similar enough that the Mandans and Hidatsas were able to communicate with one another.

Map 4.3. Exotic trade goods arrived on the Northern Great Plains through continental trade routes.

The Sahnish, or Arikaras, were also earth-lodge-dwelling people. They pressed north from Missouri River villages in Nebraska and South Dakota, sometimes coming into conflict with the Mandans and Hidatsas. Though they were villagers who also raised corn and other crops, their language was part of the Caddoan family, and their history was very different from their Missouri River neighbors. Once associated with the Pawnees in Nebraska, the Sahnish left the lower Missouri River in the fifteenth century and migrated slowly northward arriving at the villages of the Hidatsas and Mandans by the mid-nineteenth century. Arikara oral history tells of the migration directed by Chief Above (Neesaau ti naacitakUx) who sent the people to Mother Corn, a sacred being who, with the aid of animals, led the people into the world. By 1800, they were mostly settled into villages near the modern-day North Dakota—South Dakota border.

The Mandans, Hidatsas, and Arikaras and their ancestors flourished in the Missouri River valley and dominated this region for centuries. These were once the most numerous, powerful, and influential peoples of the Northern Great Plains until the horrific smallpox epidemics drastically reduced their populations and made them vulnerable to attacks and raids by Dakotas (often called Sioux). Their villages were major trading centers—long established prior to the appearance in this region of guns, horses, and other items of European origin. Interaction and political alliance among these great nations continue to the present day as the Mandan, Hidatsa and Arikara Nations, also known as the Three Affiliated Tribes, with headquarters at Fort Berthold Indian Reservation.

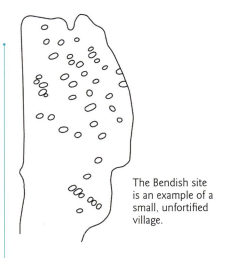

The Bendish site is an example of a small, unfortified village.

The archaeological evidence for Plains Village culture in the Middle Missouri region is very rich, revealing a complex history of interaction among the villages, growth and loss of population, and adaptation to new technologies and ideas. Archaeologists have identified many villages and have at least partially excavated several sites, particularly those impacted by the construction of the Garrison, Oahe, Big Bend, and Fort Randall dams in the 1950s.

The earliest ancestral Mandan villages, established between the early 1200s and about 1400, were relatively small and were scattered throughout the Missouri River valley. The villages were politically and economically autonomous. Archaeological studies indicate villages had from twelve to fifty-six lodges with an estimated population of between 120 to 672 individuals per village. Some villages had fortification systems while others did not. The gardens near each village encompassed between ninety and one hundred-thirty acres. Lodges were constructed on shallow pits dug about one or two feet below the ground surface. They had mat- or bark-covered gabled roofs supported by three or more main posts placed along the centerline. House construction had to be planned in advance so that the trees could be cut and allowed to dry for a year or more before they were ready to be used in construction. The houses had hearths inside, often positioned beneath the center line of the roof, and underground storage pits (cache pits) inside as well as outside the house structure. Forty to sixty posts and an equal number of rafter beams were used to build each structure. All of this timber and wood was harvested in the Missouri River floodplain. One early village site is known today as Tony Glas. This village had a fortification ditch and palisade enclosing three sides of the village. The fourth side opened to a steep bank on the Missouri River. There were forty-six lodges within the twenty acre site—about 2.3 houses per acre.

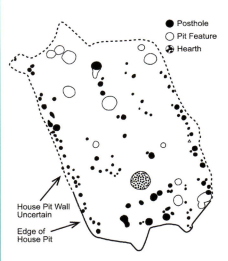

Early Mandan lodges were usually rectangular and constructed in a pit like this house at the Bendish site.

Huff village was a densely populated, fortified village. *Illustration by Leon Basler*

Illustration of a rectangular lodge.

Excavation of the palisade wall on the village interior. The fortification ditch is on the exterior of the palisade wall.

Lodges provided enough space for an extended family (grandparents, parents, and children) of from ten to fifteen or more people.

This pattern changed by the 1400s when the Mandans consolidated into large fortified villages. One of these village sites is now the Huff State Historic Site on the west bank of the Missouri River, south of the present-day city of Mandan. Huff, occupied for about twenty-five years around 1450, was densely populated with nearly eight houses per acre. The village, including its fortifications, covered about twelve acres. A modern city residential area of the same size—about five city blocks—would typically house about five hundred people; about one thousand individuals lived at Huff Village. All the lodges faced to the southwest and were arranged roughly in rows paralleling the river bank. A large ceremonial lodge faced an open plaza near the center of the village indicating some form of central social or political leadership in the community. Gardens surrounding the village may have covered 400 acres. The village, excluding the gardens, was surrounded by a massive fortification system. The occupants were most likely concerned about attacks from other groups of village farmers, probably ancestors of historic Arikaras, who moved from the Central Plains into South Dakota during the 1400s.

Huff is a good example of a fortified village prepared for possible attack. The palisade, two thousand feet long with ten well-defined bastions extending from the wall, protected the village on three sides. The Missouri River provided a natural barrier on the east side of the village. About 2,500 posts were used in the palisade wall. Beyond the wall was a ditch five feet deep and fifteen feet wide. The bastions gave an advantage to village defenders in that they could see and repel anyone who got close to the wall. Without the bastions, attackers protected with shields might have been able to get close enough to set the palisade—and the village—on fire. Huff did not burn, but the massive defenses indicate the villagers certainly felt endangered.

While the earliest earthlodges, and most of the lodges at Huff, were rectangular, at least one house at Huff reveals that some residents were developing new ideas about architecture. This house was roughly square in outline with rounded corners. It had four main support posts in the interior forming a square, and a central hearth.

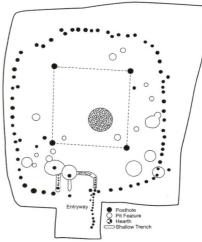

In Huff Village change in architecture was evident.

This lodge foreshadows a shift in architecture from long-rectangular to circular house forms. During the 150-year period between 1450 and 1600, both the Mandans and Hidatsas adopted the circular earthlodge, Similar house forms were constructed by the Arikaras miles to the south of the Mandan communities.

The Knife River region was mostly populated by the ancestral Awatixa Hidatsa villagers. There were scattered farming communities spread from Square Buttes (a few miles north of the city of Mandan) upstream to the Little Missouri and Yellowstone rivers. Long rectangular lodges appear in groups of two or three spread apart from a few hundred yards to a mile or so. Their villages were unfortified suggesting they were in uncontested territory. The population of the Hidatsas was substantially increasing in the fourteenth and fifteenth centuries with a few large villages below the Knife River. Other small settlements consisting of a few lodges were spread elsewhere. Villages varied in size from two to approximately twenty acres and house density is thought to have been about four to six lodges per acre. Some researchers have estimated that the Awatixa Hidatsa population around the early- to mid-fifteenth century numbered between eight and ten thousand people. By contrast the Mandan villages in the Heart River region were fortified.

Scattered groups of two or three houses were typical of Hidatsa villages in the Early Village era. *Illustration by Marcia Goldenstein. Courtesy of University of North Dakota.*

During the early 1500s the smaller settlements were abandoned and Awatixa Hidatsa populations consolidated in fewer, but larger villages. Houses were now closely spaced with a density of ten or eleven houses per acre. Some of the smaller villages were fortified. By 1650, the twelve or more Awatixa Hidatsa villages had been reduced to just two and the population may have been reduced by fifteen to twenty percent of what it had been 250 years earlier. The loss of population among the Hidatsas and Mandans may have been caused by epidemics of diseases, including smallpox, that had spread from the newly established English colonies on the Atlantic coast.

Many Hidatsa villages were located on the Knife River. Lower Hidatsa and Sakakawea (river's edge) villages are two of the sites at Knife River Indian Villages National Historic Site.

In the 1600s, the Awaxawi and Hidatsa-proper subgroups had begun a westward migration toward the Missouri River. The Awaxawis arrived first and established villages near the Mandans at the Heart River; later they moved up the Missouri River to the mouth of the Knife River. The Hidatsa-proper subgroups migrated in waves and eventually consolidated at Big Hidatsa Village on the Knife River. The 1700s saw new growth in the Hidatsa population. By 1780, the Hidatsa-proper were living in ninety to one hundred lodges in the village of Big Hidatsa, the Awatixas were living in approximately sixty lodges at Lower Hidatsa, and the Awaxawis had forty lodges at a village now known as Molander Indian Village State Historic Site.

Double Ditch was a busy, densely populated Mandan village at its founding around 1490. *Mural at the Heritage Center and State Museum in the Innovation Gallery: Early Peoples painted by Robert Evans.*

While the Hidatsas were migrating and establishing new villages, the Mandans had settled into several villages surrounded by gardens along the Missouri and Heart rivers. Toward the end of the fifteenth century, individual Mandan villages experienced population growth and all known villages had fortification systems for protection. Around 1500, Mandans constructed seven large, well-defended villages near the mouth of the Heart River at its confluence with the Missouri. Some Heart River villages were occupied continuously from 1490 to 1785. The Mandan population in this area probably totaled ten thousand or more during this time. The largest village, Double Ditch, located north of present-day Bismarck on the east side of the Missouri River, had about 160 homes sheltering perhaps two thousand residents at its founding. The population of the first Double Ditch community would have been larger than at least ninety-five percent of the towns and cities in North Dakota today.

During the mid- to late-1500s, earthlodge architecture changed from rectangular to circular, dome-shaped houses of logs covered with earth. The men usually decided how large an earthlodge would be, but women did most of the building. To construct an earthlodge, a wooden framework was erected, then covered with layers of willow branches, grass, and finally, earth. It took about 150 trees to build one earthlodge. Double Ditch earthlodges were typically thirty-five to forty-five feet in diameter and stood close together. Even as the shape of the lodges changed, some Mandan villages maintained an older-style, rectangular lodge near an open area or plaza for rituals.

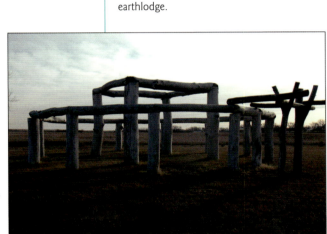

This model shows how posts and branches supported sod and grass to form a circular earthlodge.

Archaeological studies conducted in recent years have shown that Double Ditch actually had four ditches during its three-hundred-year history of occupation. The village was named by early twentieth-century archaeologists who saw two ditches on the surface, but the two earliest, and longest, ditches had been filled and are no longer visible on the surface. Nevertheless, each ditch tells part of the history of the village. As the population declined, the village became smaller and the fortifications enclosed fewer acres. There was considerable accumulation of household refuse during the three-hundred-year occupation of Double Ditch, and houses and other structures were rebuilt several times. Household refuse including animal bones, broken pottery, and ash from hearth fires was carried out and dumped in huge heaps from one to ten feet high and in previous fortification ditches as the villages contracted. These midden mounds are still visible among the remaining ditches and house depressions of Double Ditch State Historic Site.

Four large posts made up the central supports for an earthlodge as shown in this replica. A circle of shorter posts supported branches on which sod was placed to form an earthlodge.

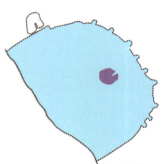

Double Ditch was founded by 1490. The Mandans at that time likely still lived in rectangular houses. The population of Double Ditch at its founding is estimated to be 2,000 or more. *Blue is residential area, purple is a plaza.*

In the 1500s major smallpox epidemics swept though North America. It is likely that the Mandan population was impacted by one or more of these. In the late 1500s the village contracted in size. *Midden mounds are yellow.*

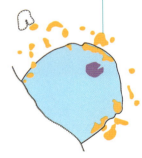

Epidemics continued to plague the Native American communities. The Mandans, Hidatsas, and Arikaras declined in population. At Double Ditch the village again contracted in size in the 1600s. *With extended occupation, refuse accumulated.*

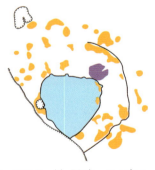

By 1725 Double Ditch was only a fraction of its founding size. The village had been reduced to about 400 residents in 32 lodges. This attests to the horrific effects of the smallpox epidemics. Between 1782 and 1785, the Mandans moved north to join their Hidatsa allies on the Knife River.

An archeologist stands in the excavation of ditch three at Double Ditch village. The palisade wall, located inside the ditch, is represented by the postholes in the level above and behind the person.

The outer ditch built by the founding community at Double Ditch encompassed twenty-two acres on a high, steep bank of the river. Built just inside the ditch, the palisade with ten bastions protected the north, east, and south sides. Villagers mounded soil in the bastions and along the interior of the palisade so that defenders were able to see over the wall and spot anyone approaching the village. This defensive system contributed to the lengthy and successful occupation of this village. However, the last and smallest Double Ditch village occupied just four acres and its palisade had only a few small, poorly-defined bastions. The population had declined from an estimated two thousand residents to probably less than four hundred. The size of the population was an important factor in village defense. A population of two thousand would include about six hundred fighting men; a population of four hundred would have a fighting force of perhaps 120 men. The village declined as smallpox reduced and weakened the population; villagers also endured frequent raids by the nomadic Dakotas. As a consequence of disease and warfare, the Mandans of Double Ditch, along with the occupants of other Mandan villages at the mouth of the Heart River, moved upstream to be closer to their allies, the Hidatsas.

The palisade at Double Ditch closely surrounded the earthlodge village.
Detail of Rob Evans painting

Life in the villages was peaceful at times, but it was not always so. Villages surrounded by deep fortification ditches and tall palisades attest to the reality of conflict. The Mandans' fortified villages and strong position as trading centers assured them many friends, including the Hidatsas, among the other tribes of the Northern Great Plains. They also had many enemies. In addition, archaeologists have noted that the late 1400s were years of drought. Limited resources and possible crop failures may have increased tensions as communities either moved to new locations where adequate rainfall would ensure good crops, or simply tried to take food supplies from another community.

There is also the possibility that small conflicts arose if a member of a community was killed or captured by an outsider or another group. These conflicts took the form of quick raids with the enemy trying to right a wrong or capture something of value, including, by the late eighteenth century, horses.

Major conflict, however, might involve an entire band or village attacking another with the intent of killing all of the villagers or taking their territory. Archaeologists debate who might have been involved in these conflicts. Since many villages were independent, but part of a larger shared culture, it is not likely that they would attack villages where friends and relatives might reside. It is more likely that the attackers were outsiders who did not share the culture and values of the villages they attacked. Attackers might have been migrating north along the Missouri River to avoid conflict in their previous homeland or to find better resources to sustain their communities. The Sahnish (Arikaras) were directed by one of their important deities to travel north from their villages in South Dakota in the late eighteenth and early nineteenth centuries and came into conflict with Hidatsas. The conflict was not resolved until the two groups formed an alliance in the mid-nineteenth century. Some archaeologists think that nomadic peoples such as the Dakotas initiated some of the deadliest attacks. They propose that because village-dwellers needed to stay near their homes and gardens during the summer growing season, they were more vulnerable to attack. If this thesis or scenario is valid, then horticulture, the very thing that gave these cultures their strength and security, was also a weakness in certain circumstances.

Ironically, raiding was often a complication of trading. A trade deal gone wrong, or one party seeing an opportunity to take goods without a fair exchange, might have resulted in conflict. Tensions increased among trade partners as European trade goods and systems infused native North American exchange systems. European-made goods such as glass beads and metal objects appeared in Missouri River villages by the early 1600s and became highly valued items.

Smallpox epidemics of 1810 were represented on several Lakota winter counts.
SHSND 79

Disease-causing organisms traveled along with trade goods from European hands to the homes of the peoples of the Northern Great Plains. Diseases such as measles, whooping cough, chickenpox, and smallpox devastated tribal communities which had no previous exposure to the diseases and no immunity. These are referred to as virgin soil epidemics. Once a disease struck a community, it traveled ruthlessly through every household sometimes killing as many as ninety percent of the residents. In 1781 and 1782, smallpox struck the Missouri River villages. Two-thirds of the Mandan people died. The Awaxawi Hidatsas lost fifty percent of their people, the Awatixas twenty percent, and the Hidatsa–proper ten percent. By 1795, the Arikaras had suffered three smallpox outbreaks. They had once lived in thirty-two villages, but after the epidemics, the surviving population came together to live in two villages on the Grand River. In many villages, such as Double Ditch, smallpox killed so many people that the survivors had to leave and find another group of survivors with whom to carry on village life. With such a high death toll, the communities lost important leaders including those who knew the rituals and oral traditions. The cultural loss was overwhelming.

Polished bone, stone, and shell were shaped into many different beautiful ornaments. Personal adornment was important in good times and bad.

As the survivors of the epidemics struggled to restore orderly village life, they were nourished by garden crops. While no archaeological or historical evidence exists to explain how the Mandans, Hidatsas, and Arikaras originally decided to add horticulture to their hunting and

Women harvested garden produce and loaded it into burden baskets which they carried on their backs to the village.
Detail of Robert Evans painting.

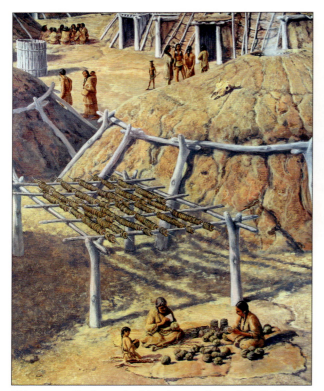

After harvest, corn ears were laid on racks to dry in the sun. Dried corn on the cob was stored in cache pits inside and outside the earthlodge.
Detail of Robert Evans painting.

This woman sliced squash with a sharpened scapula knife. The rings of squash were strung on a pole and raised on a rack to dry.
Detail of Robert Evans painting.

gathering economies, it is clear that gardening added an element of food security that became deeply entwined with their culture. Women, the principal gardeners, raised corn, beans, squash and sunflowers on individual family plots of three to five acres. Men cultivated tobacco. Life became more sedentary in order for gardening to be successful and reliable, since people needed to protect the crops from pests and maintain the gardens by weeding. Horticultural groups situated their villages near rivers which provided water and transportation. They usually built the main village on the river's high banks or terraces and cultivated garden plots covering three to five hundred acres on the lower, frequently flooded bottomlands where fertile, easily cultivated, and moist soil made for productive gardens.

Charred remains of corn cobs and seeds of various garden plants demonstrate the variety of garden crops and what villagers ate.

When corn (Zea mays) was introduced to the Northern Great Plains, it had an undeniable impact. Unlike wild plants Plains cultures had always harvested, corn required cultivation of the soil, planting seeds, and weeding. Crops were harvested over a relatively short period of time, and had to be prepared and dried for storage, but the work resulted in a greatly enhanced food supply. Over hundreds of years, women selected seeds of corn plants displaying special, desirable qualities. Plains Village gardeners eventually developed dozens of corn varieties. A woman might select a particular seed for better drying and storing qualities, or seed from corn that was better for eating fresh ("green"), or one that made the best ground meal. Corn producers acquired a body of specialized horticultural knowledge about breeding, raising, and storing corn, and they passed that knowledge down to their daughters.

Although this photograph was taken in the early 20th century, the woman is gardening with a scapula hoe as did women for hundreds of years before her.
Archives 00086-00294

Corn partnered well in the garden with beans, squash, and sunflowers. Beans (Phaseolus vulgaris) planted among the corn, climbed the corn stalks for support, and squash plants shaded the ground. Gardeners developed several varieties of beans and squash. Beans dried on the vine and were ready for storage when they were harvested, but squash was prepared for storage and winter use by slicing them into rings and hanging the rings on a stick until they were dry enough to be placed in a storage pit. Sunflowers (Helianthus spp.), probably derived from wild species, were raised along the edges of the garden plots. Sunflower seeds were easily dried on the flower head and then removed for storage.

Farming tools appeared for the first time in North Dakota during the Plains Village era. These tools include horn-core scoops made from the core, or bony inner structure, of bison horns. The scoops were probably used to gather soil, or prepare a seed bed. Bison scapulae, or shoulder blades, were fashioned into hoes, the tool that along with the presence of corn kernels and cobs provides

Gardening tools were made from stout sticks lashed to bone or antler. The broad end of this scapula cut into the soil to remove weeds or to mound soil around corn roots.

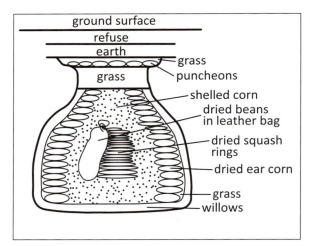

Cache pits, dug deep into the ground, stored dried corn, beans, squash, and sunflower seeds.

An archaeological excavation opened this bell-shaped cache pit.

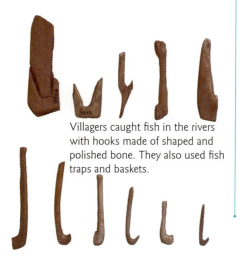

Villagers caught fish in the rivers with hooks made of shaped and polished bone. They also used fish traps and baskets.

evidence for cultivation of crops. To make a hoe, the tool maker, probably the woman who would be using the hoe, had to remove the spinous process, a protruding ridge that runs the length of one side of the wide, flat bone. She ground the broad end to a very sharp edge. The resulting wide, flat, sharp bone was notched or perforated at the narrow end in order to lash it securely to a wooden handle. The lashing material was probably animal ligament or rawhide. If the lashing loosened, the scapula was reattached. These hoes were used season after season and became polished with use.

Villagers feasted on a variety of foods year-round, and still had enough to properly entertain visitors as well as surplus for trade. Dried corn, beans, and squash were stored in bell-shaped, underground storage pits, or cache pits, both inside and outside of homes. Some caches were more than six feet deep. An average size pit could hold thirty-four bushels. Cache pits, dug deep in the ground, acted as refrigerated chambers. The number of cache pits in villages is astounding and attests to the large scale of food production. The surplus of dried garden produce was traded to nomadic, non-farming groups. Over time, the cache pits became moldy or rodent-infested. At that point the pit would be abandoned and filled with trash.

People relied on many food sources to provide variety in their diet and a constant supply of high-quality nutrition. They collected, stored, prepared, and used various plants native to the Missouri River environs. Wild plants such as juneberries, chokecherries, buffaloberries, strawberries, plums, rosehips, grapes, and prairie turnips provided vitamins and other nutrients. Plants were also gathered for medicinal and ritual purposes.

Bison as well as elk, deer, pronghorn, birds, small game, and fish provided protein in the diets of villagers and nomadic peoples. A mature bison cow yields about five hundred pounds of meat. Meat was consumed fresh, but much was dried by hanging thin strips of meat over a smoky fire and stored for later use. In addition to meat, hunters and their families utilized almost every part of the carcass, wasting very little. Hunters carefully removed the hides from the carcass of bison and other large animals. Hides, tanned or raw, were made into tipi covers, robes, clothing, bedding, and other leather products. Fur, removed from the hide, could be twisted into rope; feathers of large game birds were used to fletch arrows and darts or for personal adornment, and bone was shaped into an assortment of tools. Bison were not only an important source of food and material goods, but also were spiritually significant and central to religious practices and celebrations.

Bison and other game were often acquired near the villages, but occupants also went out on large, well-organized hunts in late summer or early fall. They camped where they had access to water and could find bison herds. One of these hunting camps was located near the Heart River in Grant County, North Dakota. It is now known as the Beadmaker site. Sometime between 1550 and 1600, a group of hunters from one of the large Mandan villages on the Heart River camped at the Beadmaker site to hunt and gather wild plants. While in camp, they refreshed their toolkits with bison bone and prepared their hunting weapons with new points.

Beads crafted from colorful siltstone were used for personal adornment.

During leisure time in the Beadmaker camp, men or women picked up soft siltstone available near the camp and crafted the stone into beads. Siltstone is a coarse, sedimentary rock that naturally occurs in several different colors. The soft stone is similar to sandstone and can be easily carved and shaped into beads. The beadmakers marked the center by drilling a hole partway into the stone. Then they continued shaping the stone into a rounded disk or a short tube-like piece. The central hole was completed by drilling through the center with a sharply pointed stone flake, twisting the point in the siltstone until the hole pierced the bead. When the desired shape and the hole were finished, the beadmaker smoothed and polished the stone. It was a slow process that required focus. Though the beadmaker worked carefully, some of the delicate beads broke before the process was complete and pieces of beads and manufacturing debris dropped to the ground. That there were so many beads made at this camp suggests that, in addition to hunting, this was a good location for a variety of domestic activities and that there were sufficient people in camp to leave some free for beadmaking while others worked at other tasks.

Drills

Village dwellers knapped points and other tools such as a drill from stone. Sharp-edged stones slid into the open edge of a rib bone to make a knife.

The Plains Village tradition is rich in cultural materials. Villagers made tools and weapons from stone, bone, and wood. While they used a variety of stone for making projectile points, they seemed to have preferred the high-quality flint found at the Knife River quarries in Dunn County. In many villages, Knife River flint makes up a large percentage of the projectile points that archaeologists have recovered. Some archaeologists theorize that people of different cultures met and socialized at the flint quarries, trading goods and ideas, and exchanging information about technologies while extracting flint from the quarry pits.

People of Plains Village cultures made and used a variety of tools from both stone and bone. Hunters using bow and arrow made bow guards which they attached to the inside of their wrists to prevent injury from the snapping of the bow string. Though bow guards, often made from antler, are rarely found in Plains Village sites, archaeologists found several bow guards made from thin bison or elk scapulae (shoulder blades) at the Tony Glas site. Holes

Bone bow guards protected a hunter's wrist from the snap of a bowstring. Some were engraved with designs. Holes drilled through the bone allowed the hunter to tie the bow guard to his wrist.

Grooved axe heads were securely attached to a stick with rawhide strips wound around the groove and the stick.

Villagers made rounded clay pots with flared rims. Intricate decorations in the clay reveal the skill and identity of the potter.

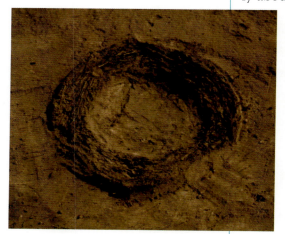

This charred coil of vegetal strands recovered on a house floor at the Huff site is a pot stand.

along two edges of the bow guard provide a place for lacing the bow guard to the wrist. Hunters usually manufactured side-notched points to tip their arrows or darts, but occasionally a hunter preferred to make an older style point for bison hunting. Hide and skin working scrapers and awls were made from chipped stone or bone. Flakes removed from stone cores could be used for many purposes. These flakes, with no further chipping or shaping, are called "expedient tools" and might be picked up and used whenever a sharp edge was necessary for completing a task. Hundreds of stone tools, or broken parts of used tools, accumulated in some houses, waiting for a day when they might be needed.

In addition to chipped stone tools, villagers also ground stone into tools using locally obtained stone such as diorite deposited in the area by glaciers thousands of years earlier. Celts (SELTs), tools with a long, narrow blade similar to an axe or hoe, and axes of this material have been found at several sites. Grooved axes have beveled blades on both ends and a groove flanked by ridges cut across the center of the tool. The blades were squared off and the tip edges were ground flat and resharpened as they became dulled by use. The axe was lashed to a stout handle and may have been used to cut and shape the trees and timber that supported earthlodges or were raised to form the palisade surrounding the village. Celts likewise were important wood working tools and often used as a splitting wedge.

Villagers made heavy tools for smashing or pounding such as mauls and hammerstones, as well as milling stones for grinding grain, crushing chokecherries, or pulverizing dried meat. The milling stone, also known as a metate (meh TAH tay), was the surface upon which the dried grains were placed. Then a person (presumably a woman would be grinding grain for food) would use a smaller stone, called a mano (MAH no), to grind the grain into flour. The milling stones were typically about two to three pounds, but sometimes women used much larger metates, weighing as much as one hundred pounds. The process of grinding grain left a depression in the grinding surface. The mano became flattened and rounded over time and fitted to the depression in the milling stone; both became polished from use. The mano and the milling stones were made from stones picked up nearby that were selected for their size and shape. It is likely that a well-shaped, properly sized mano and perhaps a not-too-large milling stone would be handed down for generations.

Many of the bone tools found at village sites are similar to those used for centuries by peoples of earlier cultures of North Dakota. Fleshers and scrapers were used to prepare and soften animal hides. Awls made from long bones of large animals or from splinters of stone were polished, sharpened to a point, and used to puncture pieces of hides that were then sewn together to make clothing, containers, or other items. Scapula hoes and squash slicing knives are commonly found in Plains Village sites; they were key implements for the work required to maintain gardens. At some sites, multiple hoes been recovered from a single cache pit.

Villagers continued to produce pottery and improve on styles and techniques they, their ancestors, and others had been using for several hundred years. Pots had become indispensable in household work, for food storage, and in trade. Pots were not, however, simply utilitarian. Potters gave them beauty in form and embellishments that came to be identified with certain villages, cultures, or time periods. Designs marked or incised in the clay and added pieces, such as handles, are important identifying traits. Today, archaeologists examine the shape and decorative designs of vessels to identify its cultural origins. The shape and outline of the pot rim (upper edge) and the designs or embellishments are especially important clues to the potter's culture and social relationships. Potters traded pots with neighbors or with potters of other villages to learn new techniques and design ideas. A careful archaeological study of pots can reveal which villages might have been in contact through trade or social relations and the way ideas and technologies infused village life up and down the Missouri River and its tributaries. By the 1500s, it appears that some people became specialists in making pottery.

The quality of Mandan pottery in the 1500s indicates craft specialization. It is likely that vessels were manufactured by relatively few households and traded to others.

Life in the Missouri River villages was not entirely about work. Gaming pieces found at multiple sites suggest leisure time was filled with games of chance and skill. Story-telling probably filled long hours on winter days. Although there is no archaeological evidence for story-telling, we can assume oral traditions that closely mirror archaeological evidence had their beginnings in the Missouri River villages (or earlier) as people recounted their history in family and clan gatherings.

Village dwellers made gaming pieces from decorated pieces of bone, stone, shell and pottery.

Ceremonial events marking the turn of the seasons are a little harder to discern, but there is some evidence to suggest that rituals guided individual and group behavior and spiritual belief. Among the artifacts recovered at several village sites dating prior to 1450 were thunderbird effigies carved from freshwater mussel or mollusk shell. The designs are typical of most thunderbird images. The head is shown in profile, the wings are partially extended, and the tail—fan-shaped or narrow—is below the body. The image might be that of a raptor, perhaps an eagle or a hawk. These thunderbirds are typically about two inches in height. The carver polished the shell and added details to the image with incised lines; one thunderbird has small pits or dimples for eyes.

Thunderbirds were carved from shell, decorated, and polished. They possibly represented a spiritual being.

A conical timber lodge in a dense stand of juniper and ash in the Little Missouri breaks. The lodge is in the center of the photograph.

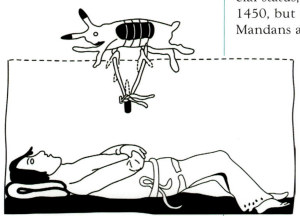

Drawing of a Hidatsa eagle pit by Edward Goodbird, circa 1915. *Adapted from Wilson, Hidatsa Eagle Trapping*

Remains of a rock-lined eagle trapping pit near a steeply sloping west face of a butte.

The thunderbird image is found in many American Indian belief systems. It represented a spirit that had supernatural powers and could bring on a thunderstorm and assist humans in warfare. At the Tony Glas site a group of thunderbird pieces was found in House 1, which faced an open area that may have been a plaza. This house was different than the other excavated lodge at the site in that it did not have a central fire pit, but had several burned areas around the house interior. It had far fewer artifacts—such as arrow points—than did the other lodge. The presence of thunderbird pieces in House 1 suggests it was devoted to important rituals. It is also possible that thunderbird images were used (and possibly made) by one person in the community who held special status, perhaps a shaman. Shell thunderbirds were not made after 1450, but the concept of the thunderbird deity continued among the Mandans and Hidatsas into the historic era.

The remains of eagle-trapping pits and sacred lodges in the badlands are evidence of another important ritual for both the Hidatsas and Mandans. Successful eagle-trapping depended on knowledge of eagle behavior, wind patterns, and badlands geology and geography. The trip of 125 to 200 miles from the Missouri River villages to the badlands locations usually took place in the fall. Groups of families set up tipis where the women and children lived while the men built small lodges of poles, grass, bark, and earth near a small stream. These lodges were hidden deep in the juniper forests where they could not be readily seen by enemies. During some days at eagle-trapping camps, men hunted bison and other big game. However, when the men turned their attention to trapping eagles, the lodge they built became a sacred place where they opened clan bundles and told ancient stories about powerful animals and eagle-trapping. After conducting appropriate ceremonies, men dug pits where they would hide to await the approach of a golden eagle (also called calumet eagles) to the bait. Pits about three feet deep, four feet wide, and four feet long were prepared in an area from one-half to two miles from the sacred lodge. The hunter made a cover of sticks and grass that hid him from the view of the eagles. He pulled the cover over the pit as he lay down to wait. The pits had to be located on the western or northwestern exposures of a butte, near, but not too close to the edge. Perfect placement often meant success. Men who waited in poorly sited pits went home empty-handed.

Placement of the pits was based on the men's knowledge of eagle behavior. In the fall, golden eagles congregated in the badlands. The raptors hunted on wind updrafts that took them to the top of the westerly face of the buttes. From high on the wind currents, the eagles would spot the bait, but continued flying to the east. Then they turned around, flying into the wind to swoop down toward the bait. As their claws grasped the bait, the hunter reached up from the pit and grabbed the bird's legs. It was a dangerous venture and men were often injured by eagles, but golden eagle tail feathers were necessary for sacred objects and ceremonies and worth the risk. When the eagle hunt was over and the sacred rites ended, men returned to their families and bison hunting. They often returned to the same site the following year, perhaps reusing the sacred lodge or the pits if possible.

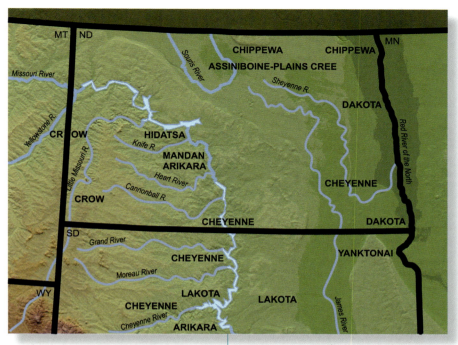

Map 4.4. Location of tribes in the late 1700s.

Plains Village cultures along the Missouri River and its tributaries were not the sole occupants of North Dakota between 1200 and 1780. Some groups chose not to make the transition to sedentary earthlodge villages and gardens. Bison and other large animals that lived on the grasslands and badlands drew nomadic peoples who continued to follow the herds and move or migrate as necessary to access a variety of resources. Who they were and where they lived is difficult to determine. However, nomads were important trading partners with the people of the villages. They traded meat, hides, and European-made goods they had acquired elsewhere for corn and other crops they needed. Late in the Plains Village period, probably about 1700 or earlier, some bands of Dakotas began to migrate from Minnesota into the Dakotas where they found abundant herds of bison and suitable places to live. They eventually adopted horses and with their new mobility they enjoyed great advantages in hunting, trading, and warfare.

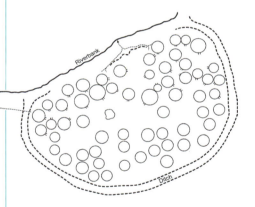

Plan of the Biesterfeldt site showing house depressions and fortification ditch.

Another group of people, probably Cheyennes, constructed an earthlodge village along the Sheyenne River in Ransom County. Like other fortified villages, it was built along the bank of the river and surrounded by a deep ditch and palisade. The people who lived there made pottery, hunted bison and other large and small animals, and raised crops, including corn, in gardens. This is one of a few known earthlodge villages in North Dakota not located on or near the main stream of the Missouri River. Yet, village domestic structures and much of the material remains found in village deposits by archaeologists suggest that the people who lived at the Biesterfeldt site, as it is now known, were influenced by earthlodge dwellers of the Missouri River

Massacre at Tony Glas

Sometime, probably during the fourteenth century, the people who lived at the Tony Glas site suffered an attack on the village that left more than fifty people dead. Most of the dead were young women between the ages of fifteen and twenty-five who died from blows to the head. Some of the bodies were mutilated after death. All were buried in one earthlodge.

This is not the only massacre known to have occurred during the Plains Village era. The earthlodge village known today as Helb was also attacked leaving houses burned and residents dead. The human remains show cut marks on the skull probably due to scalping.

Were these attacks part of a prolonged conflict between the residents of villages in North Dakota and a South Dakota village now called Crow Creek? In 1325, Crow Creek, a palisaded village on the Missouri River was attacked and destroyed. The earthlodges were torn down and 550 inhabitants of the village were scalped and slaughtered.

Archaeologists do not know what brought about the massacre at Crow Creek and they are not sure that the other massacres were part of a process of revenge. Violent conflict was not a constant presence in Plains Village life; a generally peaceful environment might have made sudden, fierce attacks even more frightening, and more confusing to archaeologists who try to sort it out today. But archaeologists work from a set of assumptions about human relationships which suggest that people who lived seven hundred years ago were violent or peaceful or both and not so different from people today.

region. The pottery is especially important in identifying the cultural antecedents of this village. The rounded pots have rim forms similar to those of the Arikaras. However, decorations on the vessels are similar to designs common to pottery-makers of the Late Woodland tradition in Minnesota. The Cheyenne villagers appear to have come in contact with people from whom they learned other lifestyles. They chose and adopted elements of those cultures that they admired and found useful, including the sedentary lifeways of Plains Village cultures. Among the materials found at the village are points and other tools of Knife River flint. Working the flint quarries would have put them in contact with the Mandans, Hidatsas, and Arikaras of the Missouri River villages from whom they would have learned much about village life and cultivating crops.

Biesterfeldt village was likely occupied from about 1724 to 1790 at the latest. Several sources, including oral traditions of Dakota tribes, identify the village occupants as Cheyennes. This was the only time in Cheyenne history that they lived in an earthlodge village and engaged in a mixed economy of both horticulture and hunting. Some archaeologists have presented the idea that the people of Biesterfeldt migrated west into North Dakota from the forests of Minnesota and found a way of life that they found to be prosperous and comfortable. Though they successfully adapted to Plains Village culture, they apparently left the village and sedentary culture behind by the end of the 18th century and moved farther out into the Great Plains to return to a life of nomadic hunting and gathering. No one knows why this adaptive change happened. The Ojibwe claimed in 1798 that they had burned Biesterfeldt to the ground, but archaeological evidence does not show that the village burned. However, the village may have endured a hostile attack severe enough to cause the Cheyennes to think about the shortcomings of village life and move on.

A Biesterfeldt potter embedded a trade bead in the lip of this pot.

Potters at Biesterfeldt sometimes pressed European-made glass beads into the clay at the rounded shoulder of the pot before firing. It was not unusual for American Indians to trade for European goods and then use them differently than originally intended. Mirrors were incorporated into decorative items rather than used to reflect a person's image. Strips from metal goods of iron, copper, and brass were reshaped into projectile points. Some tools, however, such as knives or metal bladed hoes, were quite useful just as they were made.

The beads used by Biesterfeldt potters serve as a reminder that European and European-American traders and trade goods had become embedded in the economies of Northern Great Plains cultures. Trade goods and European trade practices generated increased tensions among near and distant trading partners that rippled through American Indian communities from the east coast into the Great Lakes region and onto the Great Plains. Tribes sought to secure positions of power as middle-men in regional trade involving local and European goods. The impact of trade may have caused increasingly powerful bands of Dakotas and other tribes who sought to position themselves at the center of the trading system to push the Cheyennes out of the region.

The arrival and introduction of horses on the Northern Great Plains may have been another factor in the out-migration of the Cheyennes. The Cheyennes might have chosen to desert village life for what might have appeared to be greater security in a nomadic and mobile life supported by horses.

Horses changed life on the Northern Great Plains as much as the cultivation of corn. Though early horses (*Equus* spp.) lived in North America when people first migrated onto the continent, these dog-sized animals were hunted for food, not domesticated for work as beasts of burden. They became extinct around ten thousand years ago. Centuries later, in 1519, Spanish explorers brought larger, modern horses to the American Southwest and Great Plains, but only slowly did the herds build and spread northward through the continent. Horses were adopted by southern Plains Indians after 1680, and herds continued to expand and spread to other cultures through both trading and raiding. However, horses were slow to reach the northern regions of the Plains. Harsh winters required horse owners to locate supplemental feed for horses. Nevertheless, grassland pastures and forage proved a good natural environment for horses. People of several cultures, including Dakotas and Cheyennes, saw advantages in horse ownership. They developed ways to care for horses year-round and adapted their community life and economies to their ever-growing herds. By approximately 1750, horses had become a mainstay of life for some cultural groups on the Northern Plains.

Late in the Village era, horses came to the Northern Plains and became an important part of daily life. Lakota winter count, SHSND 791

Lewis and Clark entering Black Cats Village at the confluence of the Missouri and Knife rivers in 1804.
Illustration by Andrew Knudson

Village dwellers also incorporated horses into their lifeways. Horses were useful in bison hunting and for travel over distances to acquire desirable stone for tools, to visit relatives, or to trade. The Sahnish acquired horses on the Southern Plains and brought them north for both their own herds and to trade. Horses gave hunters greater speed, could pack far heavier loads than dogs could manage, and enhanced the military agility of mounted warriors. Horses brought more tribes onto the Plains, increasing the population and creating new prosperity for all tribes.

Horses, however, taxed the region's natural resources. Horses grazed heavily on vegetation along streams and rivers. In the Missouri River villages, women had to prevent horses from destroying corn crops and trampling the gardens. The larger the horse herd, the greater the impact on the natural environment, which might have forced nomadic communities to move more often in search of more feed or forage. While the horse trade proved profitable, and the harnessed power of the horse added comfort to the lives of Great Plains peoples, there were significant concerns that horses could also pose a threat to the well-being of the community.

Horticulture, horses, permanent villages, diseases, migrations, and the arrival of traders and explorers of European cultures mark the Plains Village period as a time of complex and rapid change for the peoples who lived on the Northern Great Plains. While it may seem that there were more and faster changes in the traditions of the Plains Village era than during the earlier Plains Paleoindian, Archaic, or Woodland eras, that may be due to dense human populations and lower impact by erosive forces of time leaving much more material available to archaeologists. The peoples of the Plains Village era were, however, much like their ancestors in that they continued to practice traditional useful skills and technologies while adopting new ways that improved their lives.

As the eighteenth century drew to a close, the prosperity and hospitality of the village dwellers were well-known to Plains nomads as well as the English and French explorers and traders who came to the Northern Great Plains in ever-increasing numbers. The Mandan villages were noted on eighteenth-century maps of North America published in London and New York. Explorers Meriwether Lewis and William Clark, commissioned by President Thomas Jefferson to map the Missouri River in 1804, knew they would meet with horticultural tribes along the Missouri River and expected to trade for the food they needed to endure a winter on the Northern Great Plains.

In 1832, George Catlin painted a scene in Four Bears' (Mató-Tópe) lodge. A metal pot hangs from an iron tripod. Four Bears' family has incorporated trade goods into their home life. *SHSND 15084*

The smallpox epidemic of 1781–1782 marks the end of the Plains Village period. Throughout the following seven decades, the Mandans, Hidatsas, and Arikaras endured more epidemics, more conflicts with nomadic peoples, and more intense and culturally disturbing encounters with non-Indians. Earthlodges, pottery, and stone points eventually gave way to log and frame houses, and metal utensils, tools, and weapons. As changes continued to disturb and change the lifeways of the people of the villages, the Hidatsas, Arikaras, and Mandans adapted again to new social and political circumstances while holding on to cultural values and traditions that had served them well.

A detail of Robert Evans painting of Double Ditch in the Innovation Gallery: Early Peoples at the North Dakota Heritage Center and State Museum.

Plains Village Period Timeline
AD 1200 to 1850

	NORTH DAKOTA	NORTH AMERICA	WORLD
AD 1850	1845 Like-A-Fishhook Site	Congress passes Indian Removal Act	Irish potato famine
AD 1800	Arikaras settle in Mitu'tahakto's Smallpox epidemic	American Fur Company Corps of Discovery American War of Independence	Napoleon invades Egypt
AD 1750	Horses common on the Northern Plains Biesterfeldt Site	Iroquois Confederacy Smallpox vaccination, Boston	First British innoculation against smallpox
AD 1700	Hidatsa villages at Knife River region; Mandans join Hidatsas at Knife River region late 1700s	Plymouth Colony	
AD 1650			
AD 1600	Mandan villages at Heart River region		Shakespeare is writing plays Ivan the Terrible becomes Czar of the Russian Empire Portugal begins intercontinental trade of African slaves
AD 1550		Spanish conquistadors in modern-day New Mexico Horses return to North America Columbus lands on the Caribbean island	Smallpox decimates Inca in Peru
AD 1500			
AD 1450	Huff Site	Aztec Empire, Mesoamerica 1300-1520	Gutenberg invents printing press
AD 1400			
AD 1350		Little Ice Age ca. 1300-1850	"Black death" epidemic, Europe
AD 1300	Numerous early villages along the Missouri River		Renaissance Period, Europe 1300-1600
AD 1250	Tony Glas Site	Cahokia - larger than London in 1250 Mississippian Culture 800-1600	Inca Empire, South America 1250-1580

TRACES ▶ EARLY PEOPLES OF NORTH DAKOTA | 91

Oral Tradition

Bones, stones, pottery are important pieces of evidence that archaeologists use to determine how people lived in the past. Through years of analysis and discussion, archaeologists have extracted many details about the people who for generations worked and raised their families on the Northern Great Plains. However, there are still many aspects of the history of the ancient past that can only be understood with words. These might include questions about thoughts and beliefs. Oral tradition is one resource that can address some of those unanswered questions.

Oral tradition, as the term suggests, is one way societies pass information throughout the community or from one generation to the next. The words are spoken, not written, accompanied by gestures, subtle and grand tonal changes, pauses, and sometimes insertions of song or poetry. Stories are often very long, filled with minute detail, many characters, and multiple events. On the Northern Great Plains, stories filled the long hours of winter which was, in many cultures, the only proper time to tell the stories. The story was accepted, approved, and sometimes modified by the listeners. The stories are lively, not only in content, but in a dynamic response to changes in the social and spiritual order of the community.

Every culture has an oral tradition, including American Indian tribes. Every tribe has a different set of oral traditions and the specific nature of the stories varies among tribal cultures, but there are certain conventions that prevail. There are origin stories which explain how the tribe came to be in the place they call home. These stories may include creation (by spiritual beings), emergence (from the earth, sky, or other natural features), or migration. One of these processes guided each tribe to its place on earth and instructed them to become who they are. Origin stories often celebrate the important elements of the tribe's culture. For instance, Arikara origin stories tell of Mother Corn who helped the people emerge from under the surface of the earth where they had been sent to protect them from a great flood, and instructed them in the cultivation of corn, a plant that nourished both body and spirit.

Another type of oral tradition is the trickster story. The trickster may take the form of a coyote, as it was for the Mandans, Hidatsas, and Arikaras, or a spirit being such as the Nanabozho of the Ojibwa. The Lakota trickster was Iktomi, the spider. Tricksters usually have super-human powers; they can die and come back to life or kill and bring the victim back to life. They can move back and forth between the sky and the earth. Like Aesop's tortoise, or the African American traditional character Bre'r Rabbit, the trickster teaches life's lessons through outrageous humor.

Some oral traditions can be very helpful to archaeologists in explaining historical events. The long-told stories contain pieces of historical information that ground the stories in place and in a long-ago past. But modern archaeologists, anthropologists, and historians find that oral traditions support other resources. Archaeologists and historians increasingly rely on oral tradition to confirm or direct their studies.

For instance, archaeologists found a place on the Missouri River where a very old village existed. The people who lived at Flaming Arrow (as it is now called) lived in oval earth-lodges. The site dates to around AD 1100 which pre-dates the Plains Village era, but it was a permanent village. The site was named Flaming Arrow to honor the oral tradition of the Awatixa Hidatsas who believe that their time on earth began along the Missouri near the mouth of the Knife River. Their origin story tells of Charred Body, a man from "the skies" who wanted to hunt bison, but the herds had disappeared. He heard them calling (bellowing) from below. Making a hole in the sky with an arrow, he looked down and saw herds of bison on earth below. Charred Body transformed himself into an arrow and flew down to earth and landed near Charred Body Creek (now known as Turtle Creek in McLean County, south of Washburn). He flew so fast that when he landed, the arrow became stuck in the earth. An evil spirit living nearby wore moccasins that burned with fire; he set out to find the arrow and destroy it with fire. The flames merely charred the arrow. Meanwhile, Charred Body (as he became known after the fire burned the arrow) formed a spring around the arrow; the water loosened the ground so he could free himself from the earth. Charred Body established thirteen lodges at this place and sent for his relatives to join him on earth where they could hunt bison, raise corn, and live in prosperity. The thirteen lodges became the thirteen villages of the Hidatsa clans.

The oral tradition of the Awatixa Hidatsas confirms and provides further explanation for the archaeological studies of the

Flaming Arrow site. The science of archaeology and the ancient oral traditions of the Hidatsas complement one another to explain how the village came to be established along the river and how Plains Village traditions emerged from Late Plains Woodland traditions.

Sometimes there is conflict between the scientific archaeological record and oral tradition. The story teller said that the people who lived in Charred Body's thirteen villages raised corn, but there is no archaeological evidence at Flaming Arrow or the later village at Menoken to prove this. This conflict troubles neither archaeologists nor the Hidatsas. Stories told through generations are flexible; the core of the story remains important while the details change to reflect changes in economic activity, social organization, and spiritual practices.

In an effort to preserve oral traditions of American Indians, the Bureau of American Ethnology sent anthropologists into the field in the late nineteenth century to record the oral traditions of many American Indian tribes. Ironically, the preservation effort had a deadening effect on the stories. When oral traditions are written down, they lose the power to engage the listener (or reader) that the same story had in the oral form. Recorded stories lack the speaker's inflection and gestures as well as the listeners' response. The written stories become inflexible, unable to respond to modernizing language and recent events. In the past, certain stories were told only by people who had the right to tell them or who held special positions, such as shamans, and could tell the story in the proper way at the proper time. These people linked language, narrative, and presentation to the living world of the community. On the other hand, written-word stories are available to everyone and add depth of meaning to the objects recovered at the sites of ancient camps. While it is to our benefit to have collections of these stories available, it is good to know that the oral tradition—alive with voice, sound, movement—continues today among the American Indians of North Dakota.

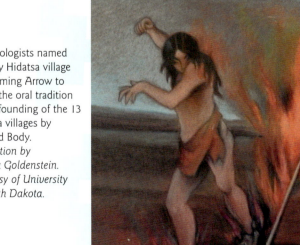

Archaeologists named an early Hidatsa village site Flaming Arrow to honor the oral tradition of the founding of the 13 Hidatsa villages by Charred Body. *Illustration by Marcia Goldenstein. Courtesy of University of North Dakota.*

Chapter 5

Bison, Horses, and International Trade

The Equestrian Tradition and Fur Trade Era
AD 1785 to 1880

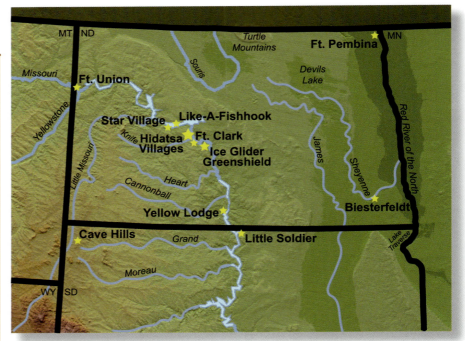

Map 5.1. Fur Trade and Equestrian Era sites.

Friend My horse Flies like a bird
As it runs

kolá mitá śun ke knyan' yan
in'yanke lo

– Brave Buffalo, Yanktonai

Horse sculpture SHSND 1115

As the eighteenth century drew to a close, Northern Great Plains cultures experienced rapid economic and environmental change. Both sedentary villagers and nomadic tribes depended on bison for food and other necessities as earlier residents had for thousands of years. Bison herds had flourished during the Little Ice Age (AD 1500 to 1800) when climate conditions favored short- and mixed-grass ecosystems. However, grass production diminished slowly as temperatures rose. Periods of drought marked the nineteenth century, the most severe occurring between 1817 and 1826 and again from 1853 to1872. The bison population underwent slow natural reduction when grass production was insufficient to support the herds. Though bison herds large enough to darken the landscape to the horizon awed nineteenth century non-Indian visitors, the stability and reliability of the bison herds would soon be threatened by a combination of natural reduction and increased hunting.

During the early nineteenth century, peoples of different cultures began to migrate into the Northern Plains seeking better access to bison and other resources. The Mandans and Hidatsas had been settled in permanent villages along the Missouri River and its tributaries for centuries. Cheyennes lived, for a few decades at least, in permanent villages along the Sheyenne River. Ojibwes (also known as Ojibwas or Chippewas) migrated slowly into the northern part of the region finding the resources of the Red River, Devils Lake, and the Turtle Mountains suited to their needs. Assiniboines hunted the Plains to the west and north of the Missouri River. Arikaras slowly moved up the

Missouri River toward the villages of the Mandans and Hidatsas over the course of several decades. The seven bands of Western Dakotas and the Middle Dakotas moved west into the Plains from their earlier homelands in the forested regions of Minnesota, Wisconsin, and Iowa. After 1865, settlement of non-Indian Americans on the Great Plains presented new social and environmental challenges to resident cultures. In the same decades, the military power of the United States became a more significant influence on tribes. Ultimately, the United States, using armed force, deprived Plains tribes of the ability to make their own decisions. Between 1785 and 1880, the cultural landscape of the Northern Plains underwent dynamic and nearly constant social, economic, and political change.

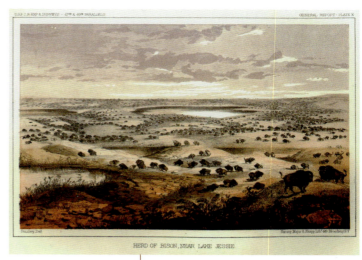

Bison once crowded the landscape around Lake Jessie, now a North Dakota state historic site.

Many of these social and economic changes originated in the international fur trade which exerted a significant impact on the cultures of the region in the late eighteenth and early nineteenth centuries. The fur trade had been changing the natural environment and social relations of North America since the 1600s and reached North Dakota by 1800. Trading companies representing Spanish, French, British, and later United States interests competed with each other to secure a prominent place in the Plains economy. Trade generated competition and conflict among tribes for access to traders and manufactured goods. The "coin" of the trade was hides of beaver, mink, muskrat, otter, and other fur-bearing animals. Tribes sought to expand their territories in order to acquire pelts and exchange them for the manufactured goods they enjoyed and were beginning to find necessary. When the demand for fine furs declined sharply in the 1820s, the fur trade shifted to bison hides, tanned with the hair on, often called robes.

These small clay horse effigies were children's toys. *SHSND 12711.1564 & 1565 136553*

An important factor influencing all peoples living in the region was the increasing use and dependence on horses. Horses began to appear on the Northern Great Plains in the early 1700s. However, they were not widely used for hunting and transportation until about 1750.

By 1780, bands of Western and Middle Dakotas were "fully mounted" equestrians. They had large herds of horses bred and trained for specific tasks. Hunting horses were speedy and agile; slower horses carried household goods including tipis from one camp to another. Traders and others commented on how quickly the Dakotas could travel from one camp to another and quickly set up a village that met all the needs of the people. Horses made it possible for the people to

Horses could carry more goods than dogs. Travois could carry very young children or an adult unable to walk. *SHSND 0739-v1-p52a*

Horses on the Northern Great Plains

Horses have roamed North America for millions of years. They evolved from a tiny, four-toed creature (*Hyracotherium*) to a single-toed horse (*Equus*) about the size of a dog. Early *Equus* coexisted with the earliest humans in North America and probably provided some of their diet. Horses disappeared from this continent by the end of the Pleistocene Epoch, about 11,000 years ago.

Modern horses returned to North America with Spanish conquistadors in the sixteenth century. The Spanish guarded their horses and few escaped. Pope's Rebellion of 1680 drove the Spanish from New Mexico leaving their horses behind. Comanches, Utes, and Apaches captured horses and developed the skills they needed to ride and hunt on horseback. Decades later, Northern Plains tribes acquired horses through trade.

The northern grasslands provide excellent habitat for horses as long as humans supply winter feed. Horses' teeth evolved specifically for eating grass. The teeth are long enough to withstand the wearing away that results from a diet of grass. In winter, horses eat tree bark, dried grass (hay), and twigs.

Horses are most comfortable in a herd led by a mare. Only one or two stallions stay with a herd. The group protects all members, especially young foals, from predators. Horses have a keen sense of hearing and a sense of vision that conveys motion quite easily. If movement suggests danger, horses respond quickly with speed, and they kick and bite when threatened.

Continued on next page

follow bison herds or to travel quickly to the place where bison had been spotted. Horses increased access to and dependence on bison, but large herds of horses needed water and acres of grass. Sometimes, horses' forage needs forced a group to move camp to find fresh pastures.

The Dakotas acquired their horses through trade, particularly with the Arikaras. They also captured wild horses and the horses of their enemies. Horses were traded and gifted within the band as well. A horse was a gift of honor and status. A man might give horses to the parents of the woman he wanted to marry to show that he was wealthy and possessed the necessary skills to support a family.

With the horse's capacity for speedy travel and its ability to carry huge loads of material goods, the Dakotas were easily able to explore lands far to the west of the Missouri River. Horses also fostered more regional interaction, sometimes peaceful, sometimes involving conflict, than had occurred during previous eras on the Northern Great Plains.

In 1809, Western Dakotas crossed the Missouri to capture horses according to High Dog's winter count. *SHSND 791*

Until the 1870s, all cultures of the Northern Plains depended on bison for food, tools, clothing, housing, and other things as their ancestors had for hundreds of years. Bison was the dietary mainstay in every village and camp. Tanned bison hides covered tipis for nomadic peoples and villagers who were traveling. Bison robes softened beds and kept men and women warm in winter. Rawhide (untanned, dried hides, with hair removed) was made into variously shaped containers called parfleches which were used for storing clothing, important spiritual objects, and dried meat. The long sinew from bison backs was used for bow strings. Horns were used as scoops, and later as a container for gun powder. Even after metal goods became available, bones continued to be shaped for use as scrapers, dice, sleds and other toys. Internal organs of the bison were used for food, medicine, and containers. Before the large-scale bison hunts that provided robes, hides, and tongues for the needs of urban and industrial America, very little of the carcass was thrown out or wasted.

Bison horn core and a part of the attached skull made a scoop for moving dirt.

Bison was the economic underpinning for all tribal cultures of the Northern Plains, but the international fur and bison robe trade reshaped that economy to its own purposes. By the mid-eighteenth century, French traders followed by British and American (meaning non-Indian traders who lived in the United States) traders brought metal tools and utensils, imported ceramic dishes, cloth, and seemingly useless frippery like glass beads into the well-established trading systems of the region. Some of these manufactured items, such as copper pots, eventually became standard trade goods because they were lighter than clay pots and did not break easily. Other trade goods were fashioned into something more useful. Many metal goods, including pieces of iron, were shaped into arrow points and other weapons. Beads became the medium women used to make intricate and artistic designs on shirts, robes, moccasins, and other pieces of clothing, replacing decorative designs worked in porcupine and bird quillwork.

Glass beads were important in international trade because they were easy to transport from European manufacturers and highly valued for decoration among the peoples of the Northern Plains.

Hunters killed bison in sufficient numbers to meet the needs of the community, but starting in the 1830s, they intensified the hunt, killing far more than they needed for their families in order to meet the growing robe and hide market outside of their communities. Increasing travel across the Central Plains in the 1840s and, after 1860, settlement in southeastern South Dakota and Minnesota disturbed bison herds. As settlers transformed grasslands into farmland, the dwindling bison herds pressed farther west and north. The native cultures of the Northern Plains responded to migrating bison herds by adapting to new locations and economies.

Among the nomadic tribes of North Dakota were the Dakotas who came to be called Sioux during the nineteenth century. Sioux, originally meaning "snake," is derived from the derogatory name given them by the Ojibwes. There are three culturally distinct divisions of Dakotas: the Eastern Dakotas or Santee, the Middle Dakotas or Yanktons and Yanktonais, and the Western or Teton Dakotas (known today as Lakotas). The Dakotas are further subdivided into the Seven Council Fires, or *Oceti Sakowin* (seven bands): the Mdewakanton, Wahpekute, Wahpetonwan, Sisitonwan (Eastern Dakotas), Yanktons and Yanktonais (Middle Dakotas), and Titunwan (Tetons, Western Dakotas, or Lakotas). There are seven bands of the Teton Dakotas. The three divisions spoke mutually intelligible dialects of the same language and shared many cultural traditions. Although each band had its own traditions and seasonal rounds, for many years they gathered each spring near the James River to trade and refresh their alliances and friendships.

Before 1780, Dakotas lived in the forested lands now part of Wisconsin,

HORSES ON THE NORTHERN GREAT PLAINS
(Cont'd.)

When the peoples of the Northern Great Plains acquired horses, they had to understand their behavior to maintain a herd and to train an individual animal for hunting, war, or transportation. In a similar way, enemies used horses' sense of danger when raiding horses. Horses became so valuable, owners adjusted their living space to keep their best horses inside where they were protected from bad weather and raiding parties.

The value of horses rose quickly on the Northern Plains. In 1805, Mountain Crows and Eastern Shoshones brought 250 horses and other goods to trade with Hidatsas. They were offered 200 guns, 20,000 rounds of ammunition, 100 bushels of corn, and trade goods. This display of wealth demonstrates the impact horses had on the cultures of the Northern Plains. No single factor had ever precipitated such enormous change in such a short span of time to both the benefit and detriment of so many people as did the horse.

Map 5.2. By 1800 certain tribes occupied specific areas of the region though they continued to interact through trade and warfare with other groups.

Minnesota and Iowa. By the late eighteenth century, the Dakotas rode onto the Great Plains to hunt bison and find a new homeland. As horses, bison ecology, and the international fur trade affected each of the three divisions of Dakotas, they adopted slightly different lifestyles. Many of the Santee bands remained in their homelands in Minnesota but expanded their hunting lands west toward Devils Lake and Lake Traverse. The Yanktons and Yanktonais established new homelands around Lake Traverse and the Sheyenne and James rivers. They hunted out to the Missouri in South Dakota and gradually moved north and then across the Missouri toward eastern Montana. The Teton Dakotas expanded their territory well into Montana, Wyoming, and the Black Hills of South Dakota. All three divisions of the Dakotas spent at least part of each year in a quest for Plains bison.

Tipsin or prairie turnips were harvested in the summer and braided to dry for storage. They provided part of the winter diet for all cultures of the region. SHSND 1986.234.63

The seven bands of Tetons claimed vast expanses of land west of the Missouri for their home though they continued to return to the James River valley for the annual Dakota gathering and summer bison hunts. As they adapted to the environment, they added new foods to their diet including tipsin (*Psoralea esculenta*) also known as the prairie turnip. They adjusted their seasonal bison hunts to ensure that they were near chokecherries (*Prunus virginiana*), juneberries (*Amelanchier* spp.), currants (*Ribes* spp.), and plums (*Prunus Americana*) in time for peak ripeness. Bison meat provided their main source of protein, but summer fruits, properly dried and stored, ensured good health for their families through the winter months.

The Santees and some bands of Yanktons and Yanktonais continued to spend most of each year east of the Red River. They utilized a variety of protein sources including fish and also harvested wild rice. However, as time passed, the Yanktonais were drawn to the Upper Missouri River and the stable food supply provided by combining bison hunting with horticulture.

A winter count tracked important annual events of a tribe or a band. The mnemonic images are drawn in a spiral fashion around the muslin. Swift Dog's winter count covers 114 years. SHSND 674

While village-dwellers of the Upper Missouri River left a great deal of archaeological evidence to reveal details about their villages and lifeways, mobile or transitory groups are far more difficult to track through archaeological research. Because they moved often, they left few clues to their presence and customs. Stone circles may indicate the location of a camp but, dating the circles and attributing a site of stone circles to a specific cultural group is very difficult. Nevertheless, some information can be gathered from a variety of sources including limited archaeological sites, rock art or petroglyphs, and written records of European and American traders and travelers. Another important resource is the tribal or band histories known as winter counts created by members of tribes and maintained for years by handing them down from generation to generation. A winter count was a pictorial history kept by a person who chose one event of each year to serve as a reminder of all the important developments of that year. Early winter counts were painted on a bison hide. When manufactured cotton cloth entered the trading system of the Northern Great Plains, many winter counts were painted on muslin or canvas. Archaeologists study winter counts to support archaeological studies of the Equestrian era.

Mobile Dakotas lived in tipis year around. Tipis were portable and could be set up or taken down quickly. SHSND 1952-5531

The Tetons, Yanktons, and Yanktonais followed a similar pattern of annual migration. Early in the spring, perhaps March or April, they set out to hunt bison. Sometimes a single band of related families hunted; other times a band might join with other bands. The association of bands in summer was fluid and depended only on the interests of the bands. The band lived in a series of camps close to the ever-moving bison herds. Horses transported tipis, household goods, and people across the open plains, moving the camps farther and faster each day than was possible with dog transports. Camp, called *wicoti* or "place where people dwell," was home until they needed to move again. Tipis, conical dwellings constructed from poles covered with bison hides, were easy to set up and take down and accommodated the peoples' mobile lifestyle. Tipis could be as much as fourteen feet in diameter—larger than the first house of many non-Indian homesteaders who followed them into the Northern Plains.

At the summer gathering on the James River, Dakota bands exchanged hides and horses for manufactured goods such as kettles.

Many manufactured trade goods were remade into other objects. Gun barrels were hammered into hide fleshers/scrapers.

Late in the spring, the Seven Council Fires of Dakotas gathered on the James River. In the eighteenth century, when British and French traders were reluctant to set up trading posts among the Dakotas on

Winter Counts

The peoples of the Northern Great Plains remembered their history and passed it from one generation to the next through story-telling. At some time in the distant past, they also developed a mnemonic device for remembering the major events of each year. This device is called a winter count, or in the Lakota (Western Teton Dakota) language, *waniyetu wówapi*. A single pictograph represents a year from first snowfall to the first snowfall of the following winter season.

Winter counts are often likened to calendars, but they did more than mark the passage of time. They ensured the community's common history and the events that bound families into bands were not lost. Each winter count keeper chose and trained a successor. Aging winter counts were transferred to a new hide or muslin cloth. Some winter count keepers made several copies.

Early winter counts were painted on hide with natural pigments. During the Fur Trade era, pictographs were painted on a piece of muslin trade cloth using pencil, pen, or watercolors. The pictographs were painted in sequence in rows, or, as in later winter counts, in a spiral fashion. The event chosen to represent the year might have been extremely important to the entire band. This can be seen when a smallpox epidemic is represented by a man covered with red dots. Other years, the chosen event might be something that was unusual or a natural phenomenon such as the extraordinary Leonid meteor shower of 1833 which appears on many winter counts. Events such as the meteor shower allow modern scholars to apply a date from which to count the remaining pictographs.

Late in the nineteenth century, soldiers, missionaries, traders, and other visitors to American Indian communities purchased winter counts from the keepers. Some keepers made copies for collectors. The Smithsonian Institution today houses many winter counts including one that dates to AD 900. The State Historical Society of North Dakota houses several winter counts in its collections and has one on display in the State Museum.

the Plains, Santee Dakotas brought trade goods to the spring gathering or rendezvous. Tetons and Yanktonais brought bison hides, horses, and leather goods to trade for guns, ammunition, kettles, axes, knives, cloth, and walnut bows. When the trading, feasting, and celebrations ended, the Yanktonais and Tetons went west on the summer hunt for bison, berries, and tipsin.

Gun flints, used to fire muzzle-loading guns, were traded at Fort Clark and other trading posts.

In late summer, as Missouri River villagers were harvesting their garden crops, small bands of Tetons, Yanktons, or Yanktonais might visit a village to trade bison hides and meat for squash, beans, and corn. These visits followed diplomatic efforts to establish a truce for peaceful trade. If the trading went well, they celebrated with dancing and feasting.

The American Fur Company built Fort Clark in 1830 on the Missouri River near the mouth of the Knife River. In 1834, Hidatsas greeted German explorer Maximilian zu Wied when he arrived at Fort Clark for a winter visit. *Painting by Karl Bodmer. Courtesy of North Dakota Parks and Recreation.*

Manufactured items often became raw materials to be reworked into something more useful, such as an awl or arrow points.

Early fall meant more bison hunting to prepare for winter needs. Come winter, individual bands of Dakotas usually established a camp in sheltered, wooded areas along rivers from the Sheyenne to the Little Missouri. The lower forested terraces of the rivers provided shelter from winter winds and snow. Game animals including bison and deer also took shelter in the river bottoms, convenient for replenishing the winter food supply. Winter was generally a period of less mobility, but if the game disappeared, the band might move camp to a location with better prospects.

One winter camp, probably occupied by Yanktonais in the mid-1840s, was located in Oliver County on a bench above the Missouri River. It is known today as the Ice Glider site. The 255 hearths uncovered by archaeologists suggest that fifteen hundred to two thousand people spent one winter in the camp. The camp was about ten miles from Fort Clark, a busy American Fur Company post situated among the villages of the Mandans and Hidatsas. Today the Ice Glider site is due south of Washburn on the west side of the Missouri River.

Artifacts uncovered at the site tell of a comfortable winter camp. The people lived in bison-hide tipis and wrapped themselves in bison robes against winter's cold winds. The people fueled their hearth fires with either wood or bison chips (dried manure). They ate mostly bison as well as meat of deer and a few other animals supplemented with dried and stored fruits and vegetables. They had acquired brass and tin pots, iron axes, knives, muzzle-loading shotguns, and glass beads through trade.

Although traders had been reluctant to establish posts in the distant and sometimes hostile regions dominated by the Dakotas, by the 1840s it was common for traders to build a temporary post in a Dakota camp. These small trading houses, including one at Ice Glider, were probably quickly built of log and not intended to be permanent. During the winter, manufactured goods and bison robes and perhaps a few other types of furs, were exchanged in a process that was profitable to all parties. The trade houses were abandoned when the camp moved out in the spring.

An ice glider was made from a polished and engraved bison rib. SHSND 4329

It appears that one or two non-Indian traders established a small trade house at Ice Glider. Plain white and blue-patterned dishes were found at the site. Marks on the plates indicate the person eating from the dish used a knife and spoon and stored the dishes on edge, suggesting that this person was not Yanktonai. Broken pieces of dishes, however, found new purpose as fleshers or scrapers once the broken side had been ground to a sharp edge by a Yanktonai woman. The rounded, glazed edge of a ceramic bowl or plate provided the woman with a smooth handle when using the scraper. Table forks were reworked into a more useful tool, such as an awl. Other pieces of metal became arrow points. Recycling and refurbishing items have long been part of cultural traditions on the Great Plains.

What was not found at the Ice Glider site suggests how much cultures had already changed on the Northern Plains by 1840. There are very few modified stone pieces, such as arrow points. The only stone tools are a couple of groundstone mauls and a mano. The Yanktonais adapted their lifeways to the new economy by using both manufactured goods and traditional tools and by using ancient skills to modify manufactured goods to make the tools they needed.

During the 1930s, John Saul, a Lakota artist, painted an Ice Glider game scene. *Courtesy of The Center for Western Studies, Augustana University*

While living in their winter camp on the Missouri River, the Yanktonais had leisure time to engage in a favorite winter game—ice gliding. They made ice gliders from bison ribs. One end of the rib was ground to a point; the other end was hollowed in two spots where short wooden sticks were inserted. Feathers were attached to the sticks. Each maker etched culturally specific designs into the flat sides of the ribs. The winter the Yanktonais spent at the Ice Glider camp was cold enough for snow or ice to form the playing field for ice glider games. The gamers sent the gliders sliding along the slick surface of the ice or snow with the longest distance determining the winner. Dozens of ice gliders, partial and whole, remained at the village after the people broke camp in the spring.

Archaeologists have found evidence that nearby, on the bank just above the Ice Glider camp, was the winter camp of people of a different culture. A group of Arikaras, under the leadership of Red Elk, lived in an earthlodge village now called Greenshield. Many of the ice gliders remaining in the Ice Glider camp bear designs similar to those of Arikaras and quite different from those of the Yanktonais. We can only speculate about inter-tribal games, but since both styles are present in the Ice Glider camp, it is likely they got together for entertainment.

The Arikaras (Sahnish), were relative newcomers to the Upper Missouri River country of North Dakota in the early nineteenth century. During the previous century, they had traveled up and down the Missouri River valley between their South Dakota homelands and the territory of the Mandans and Hidatsas near the Heart and Knife Rivers. The Sahnish had been pushed north as the Dakotas expanded into South Dakota. The Sahnish, in turn, pressed the shrinking populations of Mandan and Hidatsa peoples north toward the Knife River. These processes of territorial movement and relocation resulted in the Teton Dakotas establishing their homelands in the region of the Cannonball River where, for generations, the ancestral Mandans and later the Arikaras had previously lived.

In 1837, smallpox spread rapidly from Fort Clark (top, center) to *Mitu'tahakto's* (center) and nearby villages. Visitors to the trading post carried smallpox to distant communities.

A significant and devastating result of international trade and greater tribal mobility was the spreading of diseases that were new to the native populations. Numerous smallpox epidemics swept North America as early as the 1500s. The first historically documented smallpox epidemic came to the Northern Plains in 1781–82. Others certainly preceded it. Village populations were greatly diminished by these epidemics. About three-fourths of the Sahnish died of the disease against which they had no immunity. The Mandan and Hidatsa populations probably lost similar proportions to the disease. By this time, many European Americans were inoculated against smallpox and the once-deadly disease had diminished in mortality, if not eliminated, among the non-Indian population of the United States. Nevertheless, the disease traveled the river routes into the Northern Plains with traders and explorers. People living in earthlodge villages along the river who routinely traded at the posts often came into contact with the virus before the mobile tribes. Within a few weeks of initial exposure, intertribal trade and warfare brought smallpox to most of the residents of the region with varying degrees of mortality.

The extremely high mortality rate among the village-dwellers had multiple impacts on village communities. The Mandans, Hidatsas, and Arikaras could no longer defend themselves from mobile groups who raided villages for horses or captives. The disease took the lives of the people who knew the history and traditions of each village. Children were orphaned. The interconnecting threads of family ties, gardening, hunting, gathering, and ceremony that had made up the fabric of village life were severed. After the smallpox epidemic of 1781–82, the surviving Mandans and Hidatsas brought their communities together, seeking protection in both alliance and proximity, a decision that fostered both tribes' recovery over the next five decades.

Smallpox returned to the Missouri River villages in 1801, and again, with terrible results, in 1837–38. The last epidemic decimated the populations of the river villages. The center of the epidemic was Fort Clark which had been established in 1830 near the Mandan village known as Mitu'tahakto's (me TOOT ah hank tosh). Within fifteen miles were many more villages of Mandans, Hidatsas, Arikaras, and Yanktonais. Other groups also visited the post regularly.

In June, 1837, a boat named *St. Peters* arrived at the post. One of the travelers aboard was sick with smallpox. The *St. Peters* remained at the Fort Clark dock for only twenty-four hours, but the boat's arrival had been met with celebration by nearby residents. The gathering was the perfect breeding ground for the virus. Within weeks, smallpox had taken the lives of ninety percent of the Mandans at Mitu'tahakto's. As the epidemic continued, Mandan survivors moved to Hidatsa villages on the Knife River a few miles away, leaving their homes, gardens, and stored supplies of dried corn, beans, and squash. Even during the chaos of the epidemic, the trading post drew many visitors of different tribes who also contracted the virus and carried it to their own communities.

The Arikaras, also suffering from smallpox, moved into the deserted Mitu'tahakto's in the spring of 1838. They had lost about half of their population in the epidemic. The Arikaras continued to spend summers in this village where they raised crops and traded at Fort Clark. Circumstances, including attacks by the Teton Dakotas, led them to move fifty miles upriver and establish Star Village in 1861. The following year they joined the Mandans and Hidatsas on the east side of the Missouri River at Like-A-Fishhook Village.

Mobile groups were able to avoid the worst consequences of the smallpox epidemics of 1781–82 and 1837–38. Mounted and aggressive, they raided the villages and attempted to control villagers' access to trade. Dakotas were successful in confining the village-dwellers of the Heart and Knife rivers to a more restricted area while continuing to apply pressure on the Arikaras who eventually allied with the Mandans and Hidatsas as they sought to protect themselves against the Dakotas. Archaeologists have found evidence that some bands of Dakotas sheltered

High Dog, a Teton Dakota winter count keeper drew a picture of the serious outbreak of smallpox in 1837. Aaron Beede wrote about this image: "Small pox carried off to 'Wanagi'yakonpi' many of the suffering people. I have heard tales of this terrible winter too pitiable to record." Smallpox took a heavy toll among the Lakotas, but it was even harder on the Mandans, Hidatsas, and Arikaras. The smallpox outbreaks of 1781, 1801, and 1837 weakened the earthlodge villages so much that the Dakotas were able to assert complete control over trade. *SHSND 791 detail*

Western Dakotas placed a high social and economic value on raiding and warfare. *SHSND 9380.2*

in the Cave Hills in northwestern South Dakota. From this remote camp, Dakotas rode out to hunt bison and raid their enemies' villages. These caves had been used by peoples of various cultures for thousands of years. However, archaeologists have found in the caves steel arrow points and brass rings as well as petroglyphs showing men on horseback demonstrating that nomadic people, probably Dakotas, camped here in the eighteenth and nineteenth centuries.

The Western Dakotas or Tetons placed a high social and economic value on raiding and warfare. Each man was expected to prove his courage and devotion to his family through success in war. A courageous warrior rose in social status in his community and his wife and family shared that status. War might mean a full engagement with an enemy, or it might mean a raid conducted by a small group of men for a specific purpose such as taking horses, robes, or counting coup on (touching) an enemy. Respect for war and warriors placed the Tetons in a nearly constant state of war.

Western Dakotas and other peoples of the Northern Great Plains traded for guns which increased the frequency and mortality of conflict. *SHSND 680*

The Tetons lived in bands (*tiyospaye*) of related families. The seven bands—Minneconjou, Hunkpapa, Sans Arc, Blackfeet, Brulé, Oglala, and Two Kettles—often lived and traveled separately, but reunited as a whole or in small groups when it suited them or for special events such as the annual Sun Dance ritual or the rendezvous gathering on the James River each spring. The adult men of each band chose a leader who may have inherited leadership status, but he could continue in the position only if he exhibited the qualities required of a leader. Tetons honored courage in war and in their leaders, but the leader also had to be generous, kind, and calm in the face of adversity. He had to put the well-being of the people ahead of his own interests. The leader did not command the obedience of the group, but he appointed subordinate leaders to maintain order in camp, in hunts, and in war. If the leader lost the respect of the people, he could be deposed.

The band's leader had an important role in trade as well as war. Historical accounts suggest that Dakotas used their reputation as fierce warriors to gain an advantage in trade. The band's leader, known as "chief" to the European and American traders, led the trading process. He appointed two or three men to maintain order and to guard the trade goods. Trading negotiations usually began with a tense encounter or confrontation and at least the suggestion of violence if the Dakotas did not get the deal they wanted. If the Dakotas found an opposing trading house was offering a better price for hides or meat, they would force a trader to offer a better deal by appearing at the post prepared for war and making threatening speeches. Traders might diffuse the tension by offering whiskey or better terms of trade. Dakotas were sometimes able to manipulate the trade in their favor as their power expanded in the Northern Plains, but both parties in the exchange usually acquired what they wanted.

In the early nineteenth century, the Dakotas sought to monopolize most of the trade in furs or bison hides and meat. They watched for traders traveling up the Missouri River from trading centers in Saint Louis and tried to prevent them from reaching the villages of the Mandans and Hidatsas. They wanted both to control trade in the region to their own advantage and to prevent their enemies from acquiring guns and ammunition from traders.

Though Dakotas hunted bison and other game with bow and arrow as late as the mid-nineteenth century, they used guns in warfare. The first guns appear to have entered the Northern Plains through trade routes in the Great Lakes and the Red River valley. Early trade guns were muzzle-loading, smoothbore (unrifled barrel) long guns. French-Canadian traders called the long gun "fusee," (fyoo ZEE) a word derived from the French term, *fusil*. The same type of gun was known in the United States as a musket. Dakotas became adept shooters and gunsmiths, even rebuilding damaged guns when necessary.

Originally manufactured in Pennsylvania around 1840 this flintlock rifle was acquired through trade and later repaired with wood and rawhide. *SHSND 292*

The northward-flowing Red River was a major trade route. Many tribes found good hunting there, but it was not as densely occupied as the Missouri River valley. Canada-based fur companies established posts along the Red River and, around 1790, Chippewas (Ojibwes) began visiting the broad, flat valley regularly to trade and hunt. They were already acquainted with the Plains to the west. Throughout the eighteenth century, they had visited the Mandan villages to trade, and, in alliance with Plains Cree and Assiniboine bands, the Chippewas had fought against the Hidatsas and Cheyennes.

Chippewas did not adopt horses and horse culture as quickly as did the Dakotas. Even after 1750, when the Dakotas were well-adapted to horse culture, Chippewas continued to travel on foot and by canoe. These ancient modes of transportation were more useful in the forests where the Chippewas hunted, fished, and gathered wild rice and other plants. The homelands of the Chippewas continued to be centered in western Minnesota until the late eighteenth century.

In 1797, Chippewas faced an important economic crisis. Beaver populations in the forests had been severely diminished by disease. Chippewas had to diversify their economies in order to survive. They continued seasonal hunting and trapping for the fur trade, but joined with their allies, the Plains Crees, on their winter bison hunts on the prairies to supply meat for their own use. Some Chippewa bands and families preferred bison hunting and these families did not return to the forests. They established new homelands along the Lower Red River (in North Dakota), near Devils Lake, and in the Souris (Mouse) River basin. As the beaver population declined due to over-hunting and loss of habitat, bison hunting grew in importance for Plains Chippewas.

The few Chippewas who lived on the Plains became accustomed to Plains lifeways and acquired horses which made them more efficient hunters. The security of their economic cycle of bison hunting and trading brought more Chippewa families to the Plains through the 1820s and 1830s. However, the numbers of Chippewas on the Plains and their strong position in the fur trade caused tension in the Chippewas' trade relations with the Mandans. Chippewas also encountered more conflict with Dakotas over bison hunting ranges.

Plains Chippewas adapted to the Plains environment but chose to live in the forests of the Hair Hills near Pembina and the Turtle Mountains.

The Chippewas were pressured on the eastern edge of their territory by increasing settlement of non-Indians who wanted to exclude native peoples from these lands. In 1817, Chippewas ceded their claim to the Lower Red River valley (northern end of the valley) to Scottish Lord Selkirk who brought Scottish crofters to the valley to farm (just north of Pembina). Chippewa hunters provided bison meat to the Selkirk settlers in their first years when the Scots were unable to provide themselves with sufficient food supplies. As the Chippewas lost their lands in the east, they stretched the range of their travels to Fort Union (located at the confluence of the Yellowstone and Missouri rivers) for trade and into southern Saskatchewan for hunting.

The Chippewas who lived on the Northern Great Plains developed an identity distinct from the Ojibwes who remained in Minnesota and from the Crees with whom they had intermarried. They were now known as the Turtle Mountain band (*Mikkinakk Waci Winiwak*), but they retained close ties to their Ojibwe (Anishinaabe) relatives in Minnesota. After the 1837 smallpox epidemic severely reduced the population of the Crees and Assiniboines, the Turtle Mountain Chippewas became the dominant tribe in northern North Dakota.

As bison hunting became more and more important in the Chippewas' economy, they undertook major hunts during the summer and fall. The summer hunt allowed the Chippewas to get enough meat for summer needs and to store some for winter. The fall hunt secured their meat supply for winter and hides for the market. By the 1830s, they had given up the corral or impoundment method of hunting and now approached the bison herds on horseback chasing the animals until the riders were close enough to kill their prey. The hunt leader, chosen by the band council, maintained order in the hunt with the help of appointed scouts.

In addition to bison, the Plains Chippewas hunted and consumed deer, moose, elk, and small game. They gathered wild rice, tapped maple trees for sap which they made into syrup and sugar, and gathered other woodland plants. Their culture was a blend of Plains horse/bison culture and the traditions of woodland dwellers. In addition, some Chippewas planted gardens. They chose to live in the Turtle Mountains and other forested regions along the northern border of North Dakota where they were able to make use of both plains and woodland habitats and ecosystems. Their adaptation to the Plains environment, gave them a broad economic base.

Chippewas adopted some of the traditions of the Plains peoples including bison hunting. This family lived in a tipi during the bison hunt. SHSND A3462

Some Chippewas lived in permanent settlements in the Turtle Mountains and nearby areas. These communities were home from winter through early spring when bison hunting took people out into the plains. Houses in permanent villages were constructed with bark or reed. During the hunt, Chippewas lived in tipis. The houses and household goods of the Plains Chippewas reflected their ability to adapt their skills to the Plains lifeway without rejecting all of their Woodland traditions. They used bison rawhide to make parfleches and other household goods such as back rests much as the Tetons, Yanktonais, Mandans, and Hidatsas did. They also made, in the Woodland tradition, birch bark containers and willow baskets. Birch bark baskets could be used to store pemmican, a traditional food of pounded, dried meat mixed with fat and berries. In spiritual practices, too, the Plains Chippewas retained some Woodland Ojibwe traditions such as the *Mdewiwin* or Medicine Lodge and adopted new practices such as the Sun Dance and Grass Dance which the Assiniboines and Plains Crees introduced to them.

A parfleche was a container made of rawhide decorated with painted designs. It held food, clothing, and other items. SHSND 82.285.49

Chippewas adapted successfully to life on the Plains because of their willingness to meet new people and accept new ideas and rework them within the framework of their traditions and needs. It is not surprising, then, that Chippewas intermarried with some of the people they met and through marriage, created a new society that borrowed from both cultures. French–Canadian men who worked in the fur trade married Chippewa or Cree women *à la façon du pays* (in the fashion of the country). These marriages were not recognized by Canadian or U. S. law and some men abandoned their families when they returned to their previous homes. However, many men lived happily with their Chippewa or Cree wives and raised their children in the homeland of their

After relocating to North Dakota, Chippewas continued to make traditional birch bark baskets. This basket was painted before the design was scratched into the surface. SHSND 01190

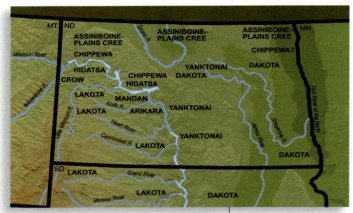

MAP 5.3. Locations of various tribes around 1850s and 1860s.

wives' families. Their children, who were raised in the cultural traditions of both parents, became the foundation of a new culture commonly called Métis. The Métis language and other cultural traits such as their music and clothing were a blend of both European and Northern Plains cultures. While they had connections with both French (or English/Scottish) and Chippewa parent societies, the Métis developed a separate identity.

Michif, the Métis language, was a composite of Canadian French, Cree, Chippewa, and English. Many Métis were fluent in the native languages of the region as well as the French dialect of Canada and English. With these language skills, they were able to live and work in various communities, particularly those of the Lower Red River region.

Aspects of Métis culture drew on their European heritage. For instance, Métis who lived in villages constructed their communities in the style of French peasant villages. Each family had a narrow lot that fronted the river and extended as much as a mile back from the river. In this arrangement, each household had water, wood, and pasture. Their one-room houses were built of log with a straw roof and window panes of parchment. While on a hunt, however, they lived in small tents.

Métis hunters were able to reload their rifles quickly during a hunt by keeping lead ammunition in their mouths.
Drawing by Vern Erickson

Métis men worked in the fur trade as *gens libre*—free trappers or traders. They had the cultural skills to enter American Indian, French-Canadian, or English-speaking communities to effect beneficial exchanges. As free traders, they resisted the control the Canadian fur trade companies—the English Hudson's Bay Company and the Montreal-based North West Company, in particular—tried to exert over all of their employees. They often had to resort to armed resistance to the large fur companies and their American Indian allies in order to maintain their freedom.

Many Métis hunters, with their families, journeyed into the Plains every summer to hunt bison. The skill of Métis hunters impressed the missionary priest, Father George A. Belcourt. He described how hunters approached a herd with muzzle-loading guns. Each hunter had one shot prepared and carried four balls of lead shot in their mouths. While riding their horses at great speed, the hunter reloaded by dropping the gunpowder into the muzzle and then spitting a ball in after the powder. A good hunter could load and shoot five times in the time it took to ride one hundred yards.

While maintaining their independence as free traders, Métis sold meat, hides, and pemmican to the fur trading posts. However, some Métis worked for fur trade companies as employees valued for their ability to communicate in many languages of the Plains. Some Métis added small farms to their seasonal cycle of hunting and trapping. In the mid-nineteenth century, when major trading cities were established in Minnesota, Métis took up freighting between Lower Red River communities and Saint Paul. They transported thousands of pounds of furs, bison robes, pemmican, and bison hides on two-wheeled carts and returned with manufactured goods. Their carts, like their culture, were distinctive. Built entirely of wood, the ox-drawn carts squeaked along the Red River Trail, heralding their approach some two miles from their destination. After 1880, when the bison herds had disappeared from the Northern Great Plains, the Métis used their carts to gather bison bones to sell at railroad depots. Unlike other cultures of the Northern Great Plains, the Métis did not have a land base beyond their small villages. When bison hunting and the fur trade ended, their economy narrowed to farming, winter trapping, and wage labor.

The Métis made carts entirely of wood. When pulled by a team of oxen, the carts carried several tons of goods or bison hides and meat. SHSND 100737-149

Métis women, like other women of the Northern Plains excelled at decorative work. They beaded clothing, saddle pads, pipe bags, bandoliers (shoulder bags), and moccasins. Their beadwork designs were much like those of Chippewa women featuring entwined flowers, vines, berries, and trees native to the Turtle Mountains and forests east of the Red River. They also interpreted animal tracks in lines of geometric designs. The distinctive qualities of these designs are the rows of colors that outline them. A flower, for instance, might have a row of red beads on the outside, and a filling of dark pink beads. Leaves were designed in the same way using many shades of one color. The designs were often placed against a single-color beaded background, on black velvet, or on navy, black, or red wool trade cloth. Floral beadwork designs identified the wearer as Chippewa or Métis. A bandolier bag, heavily beaded in traditional designs, was a symbol of authority for men and a necessary accessory for ceremonial clothing.

Glass beads of different colors, shapes, and designs came to the Northern Great Plains through the fur trade. Trading companies obtained beads from European manufacturers and shipped them to North America. The beads were small, light-weight, and not easily damaged in transport on the ocean or across the continent. Women were often directly engaged in trade for objects they wanted and had their own resources to use in trading including garden produce, wild plants, garments they had made, and pelts they had tanned and finished. All

Women acquired beads from traders, and sometimes melted them to form a bead or pendant of their own design.

The beadwork design on these sleeves was stitched in ottertail and zig-zag patterns. SHSND 9915

Chippewa and Métis women outlined each design element in different colors. Bandolier bags like this one symbolized a Chippewa or Métis man's identity. SHSND 870

Trade cloth of wool or cotton replaced leather for clothing. Though women sewed with machine woven fabric, they continued to use styles similar to their leather garments. SHSND 630, 9915, 769

This Dakota baby cradle was made from a single piece of leather and decorated with beads, porcupine quills, and tufts of feather. SHSND 4369 of these things had value to traders and the companies they represented, so women were never at a disadvantage in the processes of exchange. Women valued glass beads because beaded clothing, saddles, baby carriers, and other objects identified them as women of good standing and economic means in their communities.

Women of all the cultures of the Northern Great Plains adapted beads to the decorative work they had previously done with porcupine or bird feather quills. Quills were taken from dead porcupines or removed from living porcupines by throwing a blanket over the animal which released its quills in defense. Though the use of bird quills was not as common, Hidatsa women gathered feathers of Franklin and California gulls after they molted. They removed barbs from the shaft which they then split. Quills of both birds and porcupines might have been used undyed in a design that depended on intricate stitches, or they were dyed with berries, flowers, roots, or nuts. By the 1850s, women colored quills with aniline (manufactured chemical) dyes obtained in trade.

Quillwork was complex and took many years of practice to master. Quillwork societies among the Sahnish, Hidatsas, Mandans, and Dakotas helped women learn the stitches from expert quillworkers. In most societies, a new member presented an older member with a gift that allowed the younger woman the right to learn the techniques for making designs in quills.

This design decorates a bison hide robe. The artist used bird quills on the strip and porcupine quills on the rosette. The background design is painted. The Hidatsa artist used both natural and aniline dyes to make paints and color the quills. *SHSND 9943*

A quillworker first tanned and softened leather before decorating it. Then she softened the quills by soaking them in water or in her mouth. She pulled long, thin strips from sinew to use as thread. She then sewed rows of long stitches across the leather. The quills were woven into place through the sinew stitches. Using six different stitching patterns and choosing colors carefully, a woman produced intricate designs. Quillwork lent itself primarily to geometric designs, but a skilled quillworker could create images with rounded shapes, such as a bison head.

Women decorated almost everything in their households: clothing, blankets, bags, cradles, moccasins, and containers. Chippewa and Métis women quilled birchbark boxes in addition to leather pieces. The finest work decorated men's shirts and leggings. The shoulders, sleeves and yokes were heavily decorated with quilled designs in many colors. Leggings had side panels of quilled designs. If the garment wore out, the quilled piece was removed and attached to another piece.

Women of every culture made clothing, including moccasins for every member of their family. These Dakota moccasins were decorated with quills (tassles and vamp), beads (sides), metal tinkling cones, and trade cloth at the ankles. *SHSND 1983.425.4*

TRACES ▶ EARLY PEOPLES OF NORTH DAKOTA | 111

Glass beads probably entered trade systems on the Northern Great Plains by 1650, but they were not regularly available until the late eighteenth century. Beads, however, did not completely replace quills. Many women continued to decorate with quills, but beads opened the door to more design possibilities and a broader range of colors.

A few women made unique beads for special purposes by melting trade beads and re-making them into designs and colors not otherwise available. Different stitches allowed women great flexibility in design that included curved lines and small areas of color variations that were used to create an image or a repeating pattern.

A man who had accomplished a great deed might ask a highly-skilled woman to bead a special shirt to represent the achievement. The man would wear the shirt on special occasions. The woman's work earned payment with horses, meat, or other goods.

A Dakota woman made and decorated this leather shirt for a warrior. She crafted designs with beads, trade cloth, horsehair, feathers, and yarn. SHSND 1986.234.155

Plains women's design work in glass beads represents the high point of a long artistic tradition. Women took the beauty of their earlier work in quills and elaborated on it with the greater color range and design potential of beads. Although international trade brought great changes to the people of the Northern Plains, people used ancient skills and traditions to incorporate some of these changes into their lives in meaningful ways.

This Dakota girl's leather dress was heavily beaded on the yoke with symbolic designs in many colors. SHSND 1986.234.119

Horses and the fur trade brought change to Northern Great Plains communities much more rapidly than in previous cultural eras. One community serves as an example of the overall economic and environmental impact of cultural change in a one-hundred-year span. In 1855, a band of Yanktonais settled in a farming community along the Missouri River not far from the present North Dakota-South Dakota border. The village, now called Little Soldier, was tiny, just twelve lodges and fewer than one hundred people out of an estimated total Yanktonai population of between five and six hundred lodges. Yanktonais had become successful as horse-mounted bison hunters and their population had grown. This small group at Little Soldier, however, had apparently become concerned that their nomadic hunting lifestyle might no longer be adequate to their needs. Indeed, bison numbers were declining rapidly as the market for robes, tongues and hides increased. The Yanktonais of Little Soldier continued to hunt bison but added summer gardening to their annual cycle of economic activity. However, it was a time of drought, not a good time to take up gardening. After two years of a sedentary lifestyle, the Yanktonais left the village and returned to the life of bison hunting nomads.

Dentalium shells from the Pacific Ocean were valued among peoples of the Great Plains to decorate clothing and for personal adornment.

By the mid-1860s, the United States government had established a strong presence on the Northern Great Plains. In 1867, the Cut-Head band of Yanktonais, along with Sisseton, and Wahpeton Dakotas signed a treaty with agents of the federal government by which they agreed to move to a reservation next to Devils Lake. At first called Fort Totten, then Devils Lake, today this the Spirit Lake Reservation. The process of moving all Great Plains cultures onto reservations under the supervision of federal agents with military support continued until all the tribes had submitted. Over the ensuing decades, the Tetons resisted federal authority with force, the Chippewas resisted in the courts, and the Mandans, Hidatsas, and Sahnish resisted by requesting better conditions and access to more resources. Nevertheless, federal power prevailed and ended some of the traditional lifeways of the peoples of the Northern Great Plains. They had spent centuries adapting to changing climatic, environmental, and economic conditions. Under the reservation system, they continued to adapt.

In 1873, a federal agency was established for several bands of Teton Dakotas at Fort Yates. A few years later, probably in the 1880s, a Teton Dakota named Bildin Yellow Lodge, built his home along the bank of Porcupine Creek north of Fort Yates. The site was once a Cheyenne village and the circles of raised earth that had once been Cheyenne earth-covered lodges were visible. Yellow Lodge, following the direction of reservation agents, became a farmer. Many years later, he remarked that when plowing, he often found pieces of broken pottery that he believed to be remnants of the Cheyenne occupation. Yellow Lodge raised his family on his farm and his adult children made their homes nearby. Archaeologists working at the Yellow Lodge family sites have found tin cans, glass bottles, china dishes, spoons, knives, a coffee mill, mirrors, a candleholder, buckles, buttons, bolts, nuts, nails (especially horseshoe nails), felt hats, shoes, parts of guns, and a school slate and pencil as well as deer and cow bones. They likely acquired much of their food through government rations as required by treaties. Although they had few choices, it is apparent that the Yellow Lodge family had adapted to the new material culture and farming economy on the reservation. Their horses were shod, the family ate canned food, and the children attended school. But they had not given up all of their traditions. Also found at the site were glass beads, dentalium shells, a dancing rattle, and a bird-bone whistle. Adapting to new ways and keeping traditions that connected the family to others in the community and to their ancestors, remained the most important tradition of the peoples of the Northern Great Plains throughout the reservation era and extending to the present day.

The Yellow Lodge family very likely obtained some of their food supplies through government rations. Tickets, such as this one, recorded the rations each family received.
SHSND 381.2

High Dog's winter count from 1798 to 1912.
SHSND 791

114 | TRACES ▶ EARLY PEOPLES OF NORTH DAKOTA

1832 – A log house was built by an Indian for the first time. (A point worth noting for a score of reasons.)

1833 – This year is named "Stars-all-Moving Year". The falling of the stars in this year is said to have caused great consternation. They feared the Great Spirit had lost his control over the creation.

1863 – They slew 15 Crow Indians.
1869 – They slew 30 Crow Indians.
1870 – Chief Crowfeather died (natural death).

1899 – Spotted Bear died.
1900 – Hawk Shield died.
1901 – Good Elk died.
1902 – Bull Head died.

In 1905, Chippewa artist Charles Green painted the story of a bison hunt that took place between 1820 and 1840. *SHSND 162*

116 | TRACES ▶ EARLY PEOPLES OF NORTH DAKOTA

Plains Equestrian and Fur Trade Period Timeline
AD 1785 to 1880

	NORTH DAKOTA	NORTH AMERICA	WORLD
AD 1880	— Yellow Lodge Site	— Battle of Little Bighorn	— Britain occupies Egypt
		— First transcontinental railroad completed — Emancipation of slaves — Homestead Act	— Suez Canal opens
AD 1860	— Dakota Conflict — Star Village Site	— Civil War begins — Telegraph lines	
	— Little Soldier Site		— Irish potato famine
	— Like-A-Fishhook site founded — Ice Glider Site — Greenshield Site	— Fort Laramie Treaty of 1851 — War with Mexico — Annexation of Texas	
AD 1840	— Arikara move into Mitu'tahakto's — Smallpox epidemic — *St. Peters* arrives at Fort Clark — Fort Clark Trading Post	— Trail of Tears — Indian Removal Act — *Yellowstone* steamship reaches Yellowstone River	— First French railway — French occupation of Algiers
AD 1820	— Mandans establish Mitu'tahakto's	— Mexico gains Independence	
			— Battle of Waterloo — Spanish uprising against France — Prussia abolishes serfdom — Napoleon invades Egypt
AD 1800		— American Fur Company — Corps of Discovery — Louisiana Purchase	
	— Biesterfeldt Site		
AD 1785	— Fur trading post along the Red River — Mandans at the Heart move to the Knife River after smallpox epidemic	— Declaration of Independence	— French Slave Trade Act — Treaty of Versailles

Conclusion

Traces
Early Peoples of North Dakota

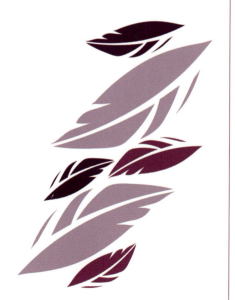

Archaeology, like history, spawns and rouses memories—some long faded. Both disciplines support a vision of people with a past that reveals the successful, mundane, and tragic sides of life encountered with resilience, perseverance, and innovation. The ancient past is only part of the ongoing story of tradition and adaptation in this long journey.

Native Americans have lived on the Northern Great Plains for thousands of years and their descendants continue to live here and throughout the country. As in the distant past, American Indians today weave tradition and innovation together into cultures that have distinct identities, with 566 federally recognized tribes in the nation today.

In the nineteenth century and through much of the twentieth century, federal government Indian policy aimed to destroy traditions that unified individuals into a cultural group called a tribe. While reservation agents effectively restricted many traditional practices, and children were discouraged from learning or speaking any language other than English, many aspects of tribal cultures were retained in the memories (and sometimes secret practices) of individuals and families. Agents, however, were not able to destroy all of the traditions of the tribes. American Indians saved what they could from the past and applied it to their new lifeways. The preservation of culture was a tradition in itself, and while the forced loss of many aspects of traditional culture was profound, the ancient values that kept families and communities together prevailed. Today, reservation schools teach tribal languages to young children, rituals and ceremonies once banned again bring people together, and efforts are underway to restore community and extended family relationships. American Indian communities are experiencing renewed vitality based on traditions as experienced in a contemporary world.

In 1940, Josephine Waggoner, a Lakota woman, wrote her autobiography and a history of the Standing Rock Lakotas (also known as Sioux). She was old enough to remember many traditions and had learned from her mother and aunts about pre-reservation lifeways. Waggoner recorded the ways Lakota traditions helped ease the rough transition to the life on a government-controlled reservation:

At the ration time, I saw them all come into the agency [from their scattered allotment homes]. Horses were scarce, but three or four families would come in together. The Sioux women were not long adapting themselves to the new mode of living. Ration days were gala days, a regular picnic, where they met, talked, smoked together, and danced; all enjoyed themselves in social gatherings as well as in talking of the topics of the day that concerned them. [Josephine Waggoner, Witness (University of Nebraska Press, 2013, p. 165)]

Waggoner's relatives and friends were not celebrating the food (rations) they received according to treaty provisions. Poor quality beef, a sack of flour, and perhaps some coffee or sugar did not adequately replace the abundant bison meat, wild fruits, and prairie turnips of years past. On the days when government rations were handed out, reservation mothers celebrated the gathering of friends and relatives and the joy of spending a few hours together. At the government storehouse, they could dance the traditional dances and speak to one another about whatever was on their minds. Ration day restored one element of traditional Lakota community interaction and broke the isolation of reservation life.

Throughout the 20th century and continuing today tribes have worked with anthropologists, archaeologists, and historians to identify and study cultural sites as well as interview knowledgeable tribal elders. Oral interviews and scientific studies of ancient camps and villages reveal the lives people led in those places and have contributed to a deeper body of knowledge and understanding of personal, family, and tribal history. In the late 18th century and 19th century, explorers, fur traders, scientists, and artists traveled to the area and recorded in words and artwork Native American life. Early fur traders established their posts near the well-known Mandan, Hidatsa, and Arikara villages recognizing the vast trade networks that already existed. Artists, including George Catlin, Karl Bodmer, Carl Wimar, Seth Eastman, among others, accompanied trade and exploratory expeditions and made drawings and paintings of their visits to the peoples of the Northern Great Plains that remain an important part of the historic record today. In the early 20th century, Northern Plains archaeologists and anthropologists such as George Will, Gilbert Wilson, Martha Beckwith, Alfred Bowers and many others conducted multiple ethnographic and archaeological studies. These classic works remain important to researchers today.

The nineteenth century artists who painted a record of the lives of American Indians show how North Dakota's cultural history is intricately interwoven with the land, water, and climate of the Northern Great Plains. This place was not simply an address, but a force in shaping the choices and decisions of the peoples who chose to live here. In this physical environment, people worked hard and raised their families. They formed communities and held them together with cycles of work, leisure, and ritual. They enjoyed good days and prepared for difficult times. They moved ahead materially when opportunities arose. And, they lived close to the earth and in tune with the seasons.

Archaeologists and others have acknowledged the regional and national importance of many archaeological sites in the state. Several sites were purchased by the state and federal government in the twentieth century for the purpose of preservation, interpretation, and research. Government ownership insured that these sites were spared from potential destruction due to housing developments, cultivation, and other construction activities.

In spite of early efforts at preservation, less than ten percent of the land in North Dakota has been surveyed for the purpose of identifying cultural resources in the state; 39,000 sites of prehistoric and historic eras have been recorded and numbered. Archaeologists have surveyed surface evidence of some of these sites, but few have been excavated. This record attests to the rich heritage of thousands of years. Only a small fraction of these recorded sites have undergone archaeological excavations. The few sites highlighted in this book give readers a glimpse and deep appreciation of the rich cultural and historical legacy extending far back in time.

The growing importance of North Dakota's archaeological sites demands a comprehensive understanding of human life in relation to the biology, climate, and geology of the past environment. North Dakota's cultural history is intricately interwoven with the land, water, and climate of the Northern Great Plains.

Maybe on that long-ago day when a group of people gathered rocks on Sentinel Butte and cached them near Beach for some future use, they hoped that this would be a good place to live. They did not know that we would think of their future as our past and that our lives would be linked over a continuum of time and space. Perhaps they never returned to that cache because the stones had lost value for them, but today, that cache of stones brings perspective to the story of human life in North Dakota—a treasure of incalculable value.

Illustration Credits

Cover

Subject	Photographer/Artist	Archive
Beacon Island painting	Greg Harlin (WRH)	AHP, SHSND

Title Page

Page	Subject	Photographer/Artist	Archve
1	Bison Hide Robe detail	SHSND (9943)	Museum, SHSND

Foreword

Page	Subject	Photographer/Artist	Archve
7	Aerial of Landscape	AHP	AHP, SHSND

Introduction

Page	Subject	Photographer/Artist	Archve
11	Innovation Gallery	AHP	AHP, SHSND

Chapter 1 ▶ Artists in Stone: Paleoindians in North Dakota

Page	Subject	Photographer/Artist	Archve
12	Clovis Figure	Greg Harlin (WRH)	Wood Ronsaville Harlin
12	Map 1.1	Amy Bleier	AHP, SHSND
13	Mastodon	Greg Harlin (WRH)	Wood Ronsaville Harlin
14	Biface – Beach Cache	David Nix (2007.75)	AHP, SHSND
14	Map 1.2	Amy Bleier	AHP, SHSND
14	Archaeologist at Beach	Bruce B. Huckell	University of NM
15	Biface – Beach Cache	AHP (2007.75)	AHP, SHSND
15	*Bison antiquus*	SHSND	AHP, SHSND
16	Knife – Beach Cache	AHP (2007.75)	AHP, SHSND
16	Folsom Point – Lake Ilo	David Nix (2013A36)	AHP, SHSND
17	Buffalo berries	Provincial Archives of Alberta	Provincial Archives
17	Map 1.3	Amy Bleier	AHP, SHSND
17	KRF Cobble	Mike Frohlich	AHP, SHSND
18	Spokeshave	Mike Frohlich	AHP, SHSND
18	Foreshafts, spears, atlatl	Greg Harlin (WRH) (DETAIL)	AHP, SHSND
18	Hunting mural	Deaton Museum Services	Pembina State Museum
19	Clovis cast, Folsom point	AHP (RC7.2, 2013A.36)	AHP, SHSND
19	Agate Basin point - Beacon	PCRG (RC4.2)	AHP, SHSND
19	Ultra-thin – Lake Ilo	AHP (2013A36)	AHP, SHSND

Page	Subject	Photographer/Artist	Archive
20	Beacon Painting	Greg Harlin (WRH)	AHP, SHSND
21	Folsom tools – Lake Ilo	David Nix and AHP (2013A36)	AHP, SHSND
21	Agate Basin point - Beacon	David Nix (2007.1)	AHP, SHSND
22	Agate Basin point - Beacon	David Nix (2007.1)	AHP, SHSND
22-23	Beads from Beacon	David Nix (2007.1)	AHP, SHSND
24	Beacon painting	Greg Harlin (WRH)	AHP, SHSND
25	Paleoindian Timeline	Amy Bleier	AHP, SHSND
27	Multiple photos	PCRG, U of Arkansas, SHSND	AHP, SHSND
27	Magnetic Map	Ken Kvamme	University of Arkansas

Chapter 2 ▶ Great Innovations: The Plains Archaic Era

Page	Subject	Photographer/Artist	Archive
28	Woman & Child Figure	David Christy (DETAIL)	AHP, SHSND
28	Map 2.1	Amy Bleier	AHP, SHSND
28	Archaic points	Todd Strand	AHP, SHSND
29	Bison	SHSND	AHP, SHSND
30	Archaic Badlands painting	David Christy (DETAIL)	AHP, SHSND
31	Bone awls	Todd Strand	AHP, SHSND
31	Scraper	AHP	AHP, SHSND
31	Rustad artifacts	Wendi Field Murray (2005.137)	AHP, SHSND
31	Atlatl throwing figure	Andrew Kerr	AHP, SHSND
32	Smilden-Rostberg mural	Deaton Museum Services	Museum, SHSND
32	Middle Archaic points	Todd Strand	AHP, SHSND
32	Pretty Butte points	Fern Swenson (32SL100)	AHP, SHSND
33	KRF Quarries mural	Deaton Museum Services	Museum, SHSND
33	KRF Quarries aerial	Mike Frohlich	AHP, SHSND
33	KRF Cobble	Mike Frohlich	AHP, SHSND
34	Oxbow points	Todd Strand	AHP, SHSND
35	McKean points	David Nix	AHP, SHSND
35	Archaic painting	David Christy	AHP, SHSND
36	Flintknapping photos	Todd Strand	AHP, SHSND
36	Chokecherries processing	Close-up of A2231	Archives, SHSND
37	Prickly pear cactus	John & Mary Bluemle	John & Mary Bluemle
37	Copper awl – Boots site	Meagan Schoenfelder (2012A166)	AHP, SHSND
37	Duncan point	AHP	AHP, SHSND
38	Pelican points	Todd Strand	AHP, SHSND
38	*Chenopodium*	Tom Peters & NDSU Extension	NDSU Extension
38	Atlatl with weight	AHP (RC7.27)	AHP, SHSND
38	Atlatl hook	David Nix (93.3.1)	AHP, SHSND
39	Atlatl weights & bannerstone	Todd Strand (14840, 2936, 7641, 6854)	AHP, SHSND
39	Copper points	Todd Strand, David Nix (3647, 2847, 11683)	AHP, SHSND
39	Olivella shells	AHP	AHP, SHSND
40	Bison Jump drawing	Museum Division	Museum, SHSND
40	Bison pound	Meagan Schoenfelder	AHP, SHSND
41	Archaic Timeline	Amy Bleier	AHP, SHSND
42	Innovation Gallery Intro	SHSND	C&E, SHSND
43	5 photos	Multiple AHP staff	AHP, SHSND

Chapter 3 ▶ Influences from the East: Plains Woodland Cultures

Page	Subject	Photographer/Artist	Archive
44	Child	Andrew Knudson (detail)	AHP, SHSND
44	Map 3.1	Amy Bleier	AHP, SHSND
44	Rolling grasslands	Brian Austin	Museum, SHSND
45	Badlands photo	David Nix	David Nix
45	Naze village painting	Andrew Knudson	AHP, SHSND
46	Naze artifacts	AHP (92.27)	AHP, SHSND
46	Pot replica	AHP (RC7.14)	AHP, SHSND
47	Pottery manufacture	Jessica Rockeman (ILLUSTRATIONS)	AHP, SHSND
47	Point diagram	Amy Bleier (ADAPTED FROM GREGG)	AHP SHSND
48	Fire-cracked rock	Fern Swenson	AHP, SHSND
48	Chokecherries	Barbara Handy-Marchello	Barbara Handy-Marchello
48	Anderson Earthworks	Michael Gregg, UND	AHP, SHSND
49	Ransom County Mound	UND	AHP, SHSND
50	Map 3.2	Amy Bleier	AHP, SHSND
50	Catlinite pipe	AHP (RC8.13)	AHP, SHSND
50	Columella shell	AHP (81.40)	AHP, SHSND
50	Copper disk	AHP (RC7.7)	AHP, SHSND
51	Map 3.3	Amy Bleier	AHP, SHSND
51	Middle Plains Woodland pot	David Nix (2011A8.20)	AHP, SHSND
51	Besant points	AHP	AHP, SHSND
52	Map 3.4	Amy Bleier	AHP, SHSND
52	Tipi camp painting	Karl Bodmer	NDP&R
53	Aerial of stone circle	Ethnoscience	Ethnoscience
53	Aerial of stone circle	Ethnoscience	Ethnoscience
53	Hide working	Robert Evans (DETAIL)	Museum, SHSND
55	Coyote, dog, wolf	Abigail Fisher	SMU Anthropology
55	Bow & Arrow illustration	Andrew Kerr	AHP, SHSND
56	Projectile points	AHP	AHP, SHSND
57	Arrow shaft straighteners	Todd Strand	AHP, SHSND
57	Fletching illustration	Becky Barnes	AHP, SHSND
59	Woodland pottery	AHP & Todd Strand	AHP, SHSND
60	Blackduck pottery	AHP	AHP, SHSND
60	Menoken aerial	AHP	AHP, SHSND
61	Menoken painting	Becky Barnes	AHP, SHSND
62	Menoken House 2 plan	Amy Bleier	PCRG
62	Menoken House 2 photo	AHP	AHP, SHSND
62	Menoken House 17 plan	Amy Bleier	PCRG
62	Menoken House 17 photo	AHP	AHP, SHSND
63	Menoken marine shell	PCRG (99.11)	AHP, SHSND
63	Menoken copper	PCRG (99.11)	AHP, SHSND
63	Menoken pottery	AHP	AHP, SHSND
64	Detail of Naze village painting	Andy Knudson	AHP, SHSND
65	Woodland Timeline	Amy Bleier	AHP, SHSND
67	Map 3.5	Brian Austin	Museum, SHSND

67	Garrison Dam Construction	RBS photograph	AHP, SHSND
67	Garrison Dam	Michael Frohlich	AHP, SHSND
67	Aerial of Like-a-Fishhook	RBS photograph	AHP, SHSND
67	Huff Village excavation	W. Raymond Wood	AHP, SHSND

Chapter 4 ▶ People of the Earthlodges: Plains Village Cultures

Page	Subject	Photographer/Artist	Archve
68	Corn	Meagan Schoenfelder	AHP, SHSND
68	Map 4.1	Amy Bleier	AHP, SHSND
70	Map 4.2	Amy Bleier	AHP, SHSND
70	Map 4.3	Amy Bleier	AHP, SHSND
71	Bendish plan	Amy Bleier (ADAPTED FROM THIESSEN)	AHP, SHSND
71	House plan – Bendish site	Amy Bleier (ADAPTED FROM THIESSEN)	AHP, SHSND
72	Huff Village painting	Leon Basler	AHP, SHSND
72	Rectangular lodge	W. Raymond Wood	AHP, SHSND
72	Huff palisade	W. Raymond Wood	AHP, SHSND
73	Huff square lodge	W. Raymond Wood	AHP, SHSND
73	House plan – Huff	W. Raymond Wood	AHP, SHSND
73	Early Hidatsa village painting	Marcia Goldenstein	UND
74	Knife River Indian Villages	Fern Swenson	AHP, SHSND
74	Double Ditch mural	Robert Evans	Museum, SHSND
75	Model of earthlodge	Dan Aird	Dan Aird
75	Earthlodge post structure	Fern Swenson	AHP, SHSND
75	Double Ditch plans	Amy Bleier	AHP, SHSND
76	Double Ditch excavation	Fern Swenson	AHP, SHSND
76	Double Ditch mural (palisade)	Robert Evans (DETAIL)	Museum, SHSND
77	Winter Count (detail)	SHSND (791)	Museum, SHSND
77	Ornaments	AHP	AHP, SHSND
78	Double Ditch mural	Robert Evans (DETAILS)	Museum, SHSND
79	Charred corn cobs & seeds	Brian Austin	Museum, SHSND
79	Gardening photo	Archives (00086-00294)	Archives, SHSND
79	Scapula hoe	AHP	AHP, SHSND
80	Cache pit drawing	Amy Bleier	AHP, SHSND
80	Cache pit photo	RBS	AHP, SHSND
80	Fishhooks	Todd Strand	AHP, SHSND
81	Stone beads	Brooke Morgan (86.226)	AHP, SHSND
81	Drills	AHP	AHP, SHSND
81	Knife and handle	AHP (92.9)	AHP, SHSND
81	Bow & Arrow illustration	Meagan Schoenfelder	AHP, SHSND
81	Bow guards	AHP	AHP, SHSND
81	Side-notched point	AHP	AHP, SHSND
82	Grooved axe	AHP (2015A.56)	AHP, SHSND
82	Pottery	AHP & Todd Strand (15800)	AHP, SHSND
82	Pot stand – Huff site	W. Raymond Wood	AHP, SHSND
83	Pottery	PCRG & Todd Strand (99.10, 98.4)	AHP, SHSND
83	Gaming pieces	AHP	AHP, SHSND

Page	Subject	Photographer/Artist	Archive
83	Detail of Double Ditch mural	Robert Evans	AHP, SHSND
83	Thunderbird	AHP	AHP, SHSND
84	Conical timber lodge	Walter Allen	AHP, SHSND
84	Eagle pit drawing	Amy Bleier (ADAPTED FROM G. WILSON)	AHP, SHSND
84	Eagle trapping pit	Walter Allen	AHP, SHSND
85	Map 4.4	Amy Bleier	AHP, SHSND
85	Plan of Biesterfeldt	Amy Bleier (ADAPTED FROM WOOD)	AHP, SHSND
86	Rim from Biesterfeldt	Fern Swenson	AHP, SHSND
87	Lakota Winter count	SHSND (791)	Museum, SHSND
88	Black Cats Village painting	Andrew Knudson	Museum, SHSND
89	Four Bears' Lodge	George Catlin (SHSND 15084)	Museum, SHSND
90	Double Ditch mural (lodge)	Robert Evans (DETAIL)	Museum, SHSND
91	Plains Village Timeline	Amy Bleier	AHP, SHSND
93	Flaming Arrow drawing	Marcia Goldenstein	UND

Chapter 5 ▶ Bison, Horses, and International Trade: The Equestrian Tradition and Fur Trade Era

Page	Subject	Photographer/Artist	Archive
94	Horse sculpture	SHSND (1115)	Museum, SHSND
94	Map 5.1	Amy Bleier	AHP, SHSND
95	Lake Jessie	Public Domain	Public Domain
95	Clay horse effigies	AHP & David Nix (12711, 136553)	AHP, SHSND
95	Horse travois	SHSND (0739-VI-P52A)	Archives, SHSND
96	High Dog winter count	SHSND (791)	Museum, SHSND
96	Bison horn core scoops	AHP (32OL16)	AHP, SHSND
97	Glass beads	David Nix (12003.1050)	AHP, SHSND
97	Map 5.2	Amy Bleier	AHP, SHSND
98	Prairie turnips	Meagan Schoenfelder (1986.234.63)	AHP, SHSND
98	Swift Dog's winter count	SHSND (674)	Museum, SHSND
99	Tipis	SHSND (1952-5531)	Archives, SHSND
99	Kettles	Todd Strand (12003)	AHP, SHSND
99	Gun barrel flesher	Meagan Schoenfelder (12711)	AHP, SHSND
100	Gun flints	AHP	AHP, SHSND
100	Fork and awls	AHP & David Nix (12003, 12711, 2011A.3)	AHP, SHSND
100	Metal points	AHP	AHP, SHSND
100	Maximilian at Fort Clark	Karl Bodmer	ND Parks & Recreation
101	Ice glider	SHSND (4329)	Museum, SHSND
101	Ice Glider game painting	John Saul (Center for Western Studies)	Augustana University
102	Aerial of Fort Clark	SHSND	AHP, SHSND
103	High Dog winter count detail	SHSND (791)	Museum, SHSND
104	Raiding and warfare detail	SHSND (9380.2)	Museum, SHSND
104	Battle	SHSND (680)	Museum, SHSND
105	Flintlock rifle	Meagan Schoenfelder (SHSND 292)	Museum, SHSND
106	Hair Hills near Pembina	Harper's Magazine (1860)	Public Domain
107	Chippewa camp	SHSND (A3462)	Archives, SHSND

107	Parfleche	Meagan Schoenfelder (82.285.49)	Museum, SHSND
107	Birch bark basket	Meagan Schoenfelder (01190)	Museum, SHSND
108	Map 5.3	Amy Bleier	AHP, SHSND
108	Metis hunters	Vern Erickson illustration	Vern Erickson
109	Cart	Photograph-SHSND (100737-149)	Archives, SHSND
109	Glass bead pendant	Meagan Schoenfelder (L-24)	AHP, SHSND
110	Bandolier bag	SHSND (870)	Museum, SHSND
110	Sleeve design	Meagan Schoenfelder (SHSND 9915)	Museum, SHSND
110	Trade cloth dress	Meagan Schoenfelder (SHSND 630.9915.769)	Museum, SHSND
110	Baby cradle	Meagan Schoenfelder (SHSND 4369)	Museum, SHSND
111	Bison hide robe detail	Meagan Schoenfelder (SHSND 9943)	Museum, SHSND
111	Moccasins	SHSND (1983.425.4)	Museum, SHSND
112	Men's shirt	SHSND (1996.234.155)	Museum, SHSND
112	Girl's dress	SHSND (1986.234.119)	Museum, SHSND
112	Dentalium shells	Meagan Schoenfelder	AHP, SHSND
113	Ration ticket	SHSND (381.2)	Museum, SHSND
114	High Dog's winter count	Photograph-SHSND (SHSND 791)	Museum, SHSND
115	High Dog's winter count	Photograph-SHSND (SHSND 791)	Museum, SHSND
116	Bison Hunt winter count	Photograph (SHSND 162)	Museum, SHSND
117	Timeline	Amy Bleier	AHP, SHSND

Archive Key

AHP	Archaeology & Historic Preservation Division
C&E	Communications & Education Division
NDP&R	North Dakota Parks and Recreation
NDSU	North Dakota State University
PCRG	PaleoCultural Research Group
RBS	River Basin Surveys
SHSND	State Historical Society of North Dakota
SMU	Southern Methodist University
UND	University of North Dakota
WRH	Wood Ronsaville Harlin

Acknowledgements

We have many people to thank for their part in the production of this book. State Historical Society of North Dakota archaeologists Paul Picha, Dr. Brooke Morgan, and Dr. Wendi Field Murray edited and commented on all or part of the early draft of the manuscript. Dr. Mark Mitchell of the PaleoCultural Research Group and Dr. Bruce Huckell of the University of New Mexico read versions of the first chapter and offered insights and updated information. Dr. Birgit Hans of the University of North Dakota provided comments and information on the manuscript. State Historical Society editors Pamela Berreth Smokey and Ann Melton Crews and Director of Communications and Education Division Kim Jondahl edited the draft of the manuscript. Though we did not necessarily always heed the editorial advice from multiple reviewers, the comments and suggestions resulted in substantial improvements. Of course, any errors in the book are entirely the authors' responsibility.

We especially want to recognize Professor Emerita Lucy Ganje for the wonderful design and composition of the publication. Her insights were important in providing a cohesive structure and drawing an audience toward the text.

Over the past several years, artists Greg Harlin, Robert Evans, Leon Basler, Andrew Knudson, David Christy, and Becky Barnes were commissioned to produce paintings representing community life based on archaeological evidence. Their art work is on display in the Innovation Gallery: Early Peoples in North Dakota at the ND Heritage Center & State Museum, as well as in this publication. Other illustrations were produced by Meagan Schoenfelder, Amy Bleier, Becky Barnes, Andrew Kerr, and Jessica Rockeman. Maps and timelines were produced by Amy Bleier. Meagan Schoenfelder was the lead in photographing and editing numerous artifacts. Artifact photos taken by Todd Strand and David Nix were a key resource. Lorna Meidinger assisted with editing artifact photographs. Wendi Field Murray, Paul Picha and Tim Reed assisted with identifying archaeological collections and site photographs.

Jenny Yearous and Mark Halvorson provided access and information for the Museum Collections. Sharon Silengo helped identify and retrieve archival photographs. Abigail Fisher photographed images of coyote, dog, and wolf skulls from the Southern Methodist University Anthropology Zooarchaeological Comparative Collection. Ethnoscience provided photographs from a stone feature site. Genia Hesser and Andrew Kerr provided access to design elements from the exhibit in the Innovation Gallery: Early Peoples in North Dakota at the ND Heritage Center & State Museum.

Neil Howe (Director of the North Dakota Studies program), Claudia Berg (Agency Director, SHSND), and David Skalsky (Assistant Agency Director, SHSND) provided much support in a variety of ways. Calvin Grinnell (Historian for the Mandan, Hidatsa, and Arikara Nation) read and graciously provided the foreword for the publication. We also recognize the vast research contributions over decades by anthropologists, archaeologists, historians, and others each building on the knowledge of previous generations. The aim of this book is to introduce audiences to complex scientific information in a manner that is accessible to the public, educators, and students.

This publication was partially funded by the Historic Preservation Fund, National Park Service, Department of the Interior; U.S. Forest Service, Department of Agriculture; PaleoCultural Research Group (PCRG); ND Heritage Center & State Museum Store, and Dr. Fred Schneider. Any opinions, findings, and conclusions or recommendations expressed in this material do not necessarily reflect the views of the federal agencies.

Further Reading

Ahler, Stanley A. 1986. *The Knife River Flint Quarries: Excavations at Site 32DU508.* Bismarck: State Historical Society of North Dakota.

Ahler, Stanley A. and Marvin Kay, eds. 2007. *Plains Village Archaeology: Bison-hunting Farmers in the Central and Northern Plains.* Salt Lake City: University of Utah Press.

Ahler, Stanley A., Thomas D. Thiessen, and Michael K. Trimble. 1991. *People of the Willows: The Prehistory and Early History of the Hidatsa Indians.* Grand Forks: University of North Dakota Press, 1991.

Allen, Walter E. 1983. "Eagle Trapping Along the Little Missouri River." *North Dakota History* 50 (1): 4-22.

Bowers, Alfred W. 1950 (1991). Mandan Social and Ceremonial Organization. Chicago: University of Chicago Press. Reprint. Caldwell, University of Idaho Press.

Bowers, Alfred W. 1992. *Hidatsa Social and Ceremonial Organization.* Lincoln: University of Nebraska Press. First published 1963.

Calloway, Colin G. 2003. *One Vast Winter Count: The Native American West before Lewis and Clark.* Lincoln: University of Nebraska Press.

Collard, Mark, Briggs Buchanan, Marcus J. Hamilton, and Michael J. O'Brien. "Spatiotemporal Dynamics of the Clovis-Folsom Transition." 2010. *Journal of Archaeological Science* 37:2513-2519.

Fenn, Elizabeth. 2015. *Encounters at the Heart of the World: A History of the Mandan People.* New York: Hill and Wang.

Floodman, Mervin G. 2012. *Prehistory on the Dakota Prairie Grasslands: An Overview 2012.* Bismarck: U.S. Forest Service Dakota Prairie Grasslands.

Frison, George C. 1991. *Prehistoric Hunters of the High Plains.* Cambridge, Massachusetts: Academic Press.

Hoganson, John W. 2006. "Dinosaurs, Sharks, and Wooly Mammoths: Glimpses of Life in North Dakota's Prehistoric Past." *North Dakota History* 73 (1 & 2).

Huckell, Bruce B., J. David Kilby, Mathew Boulanger, and Michael Glascock. 2009. "Beach: A Clovis Cache in Southwestern North Dakota." *Current Research in the Pleistocene* 26: 68-69.

Isenberg, Andrew C. 2000. *The Destruction of the Bison: An Environmental History, 1750-1920.* Cambridge: Cambridge University Press.

Loendorf, Lawrence. 1991. "Pretty Butte Site (32SL100): The End of the Paleo-Indian Tradition in North Dakota." *North Dakota History* 58 (1): 6-15.

Michlovic, Michael G., George R. Holley, Rinita A. Dalan, and Erik Gooding. 2016. "The Cheyenne Migration and the Biesterfeldt Site Revisited." *Plains Anthropologist* 61 (275): 5-24.

Michlovic, Michael G. and Garry L. Running, IV. 2005. "Archeology and Paleoenvironment at the Rustad Site (32RI775)." *Plains Anthropologist,* Memoir 37 50:196.

Mitchell, Mark D. 2013. *Crafting History in the Northern Plains: A Political Economy of the Heart River Region, 1400-1750.* Tucson: The University of Arizona Press, Tucson.

Schneider, Fred. 1991. "Stereotypes, Myths, and North Dakota Prehistory." *North Dakota History* 58 (1): 16-27.

Schneider, Mary Jane. 1986. *North Dakota Indians: An Introduction*. Dubuque: Kendall/Hunt Publishing Company.

Severson, Kieth E. and Carolyn Hull Sieg. 2006. *The Nature of Eastern North Dakota: Pre-1880 Historical Ecology*. Fargo: North Dakota Institute for Regional Studies.

Sturtevant, William C. and Raymond J. DeMallie, eds. 2001. *Handbook of the North American Indians*. Vol 13, Parts 1 & 2, Plains. Washington, D.C: Smithsonian Institution.

Thiessen, Thomas D. 1995. "The Bendish Site (32MO2)." *North Dakota Archaeology* 6.

Waggoner, Josephine. 2013. *Witness: A Hunkpapha Historian's Strong-Heart Song of the Lakotas*. Ed. by Emily Levine. Lincoln: University of Nebraska Press.

Warner, Kathryn Drennan, ed. 2011. "An Overview of Yanktonai Archaeology in the Dakotas." *South Dakota Archaeology* 27.

Weitzner, Bella, ed. 1979. "Notes on the Hidatsa Indians Based on Data Recorded by the Late Gilbert L. Wilson." *American Museum of Natural History, Anthropological Papers*. 56 (2).

Wilson, Gilbert L. 1987. *Buffalo Bird Woman's Garden: The Classic Account of Hidatsa American Indian Gardening Techniques*. Minneapolis: Minnesota Historical Society Press.

Wilson, Gilbert L. 1928. "Hidatsa Eagle Trapping." *American Museum of Natural History, Anthropological Papers*. 30: 4. Reprint. Lincoln: J & L Reprint Company.

Wood, W. Raymond. 1971. "Biesterfeldt: A Post Contact Coalescent Site on the Northeastern Plains." *Smithsonian Contributions to Anthropology* 15.

Wood, W. Raymond. 1967. *An Interpretation of Mandan Culture History*. Washington, D.C: Smithsonian Institution Bureau of American Ethnology, Bulletin 198.

Wood, W. Raymond. 1999. "The Tony Glas Site 32EM3." *North Dakota Archaeology* 7.

Wood, W. Raymond, ed. 1986. *Papers in Northern Plains History and Ethnohistory*. Sioux Falls: South Dakota Archaeological Society, Special Publication No. 10.

Wood, W. Raymond, William J. Hunt, Jr., and Randy H. Williams. 2011. *Fort Clark and its Indian Neighbors: A Trading Post on the Upper Missouri*. Norman: University of Oklahoma Press.